Better Locati
Shooting

Better Location Shooting

Techniques for Video Production

Paul Martingell

AMSTERDAM • BOSTON • HEIDELBERG • LONDON • NEW YORK • OXFORD
PARIS • SAN DIEGO • SAN FRANCISCO • SINGAPORE • SYDNEY • TOKYO

Focal Press is an imprint of Elsevier

Focal Press is an imprint of Elsevier
30 Corporate Drive, Suite 400, Burlington, MA 01803, USA
Linacre House, Jordan Hill, Oxford OX2 8DP, UK

Library of Congress Cataloging-in-Publication Data
Application submitted

British Library Cataloguing-in-Publication Data
A catalogue record for this book is available from the British Library.

ISBN: 978-0-240-81003-4

For information on all Focal Press publications visit our website at www.elsevierdirect.com

08 09 10 11 5 4 3 2 1

Typeset by Charon Tec Ltd., A Macmillan Company (www.macmillansolution.com)

Printed in the United States of America

Contents

CONTENTS

CONTENTS

Acknowledgements

The author would like to thank all the people and companies below who helped with technical information, supplied images which are reproduced with their kind permission or in reviewing the book and added relevant comments and information which helped the final version of this book.

Cirrolite UK, C/O David Morphy

Who distribute Dedo and Kino flow lights, lens-lites, Barfly lights and others

www.cirrolite.com

Polecam, C/O Mel

Who provide the Polecam system

www.polecam.com

Tiffen, C/O Danny Hallett

Who provided information and images for their range of Steadicams

www.tiffen-europe.com

Red camera system, C/O Jon

Who provided stills of the Red camera

www.red.com

Panasonic UK

Who provided images of their video cameras

SONY broadcast

Who provided images of their video cameras

Reviewers of the final draft of the book

James Joyce and Osder in the U.S., Ian Wagdin and Graham Howe in the U.K.

Freelance crew members who helped with relevant information

Nigel Francis, Ian Birch, Ramzi Bedj-Bedj and Justin Craig, all sound recordists in the U.K.

Dave and Richard Longstaff, Steve Smith, Adrian Pinsent, Paul Dickie, all lighting cameramen in the U.K.

Film & TV Lighting Services UK

www.ftvs.co.uk

Pelican cases

www.peliproducts.co.uk

Dan Oliver of Physical Fix for all the sports physio information (and for keeping my back sorted out after hard shoots)

www.physicalfix.co.uk

And my two sons Sam and Peter who patiently posed for photos to illustrate this book.

Introduction

This book has been written because I have seen many video training manuals and self-help books which do not seem to have anything to do with a video cameraman's normal working day in the real world. There are a lot of good training books for video camera work with a leaning toward the technical side of the job. Focal Press have quite a few to choose from by well-respected

NARRATION

"Location shooting at its best, the author in Iceland shooting on DigiBetacam.

authors and they will help supplement your studies or if you are already in the TV business, it will give you more information about areas you are not sure of.

But there's no point knowing everything technical about CCDs (charged couple devices), pixels and color temperatures when you can't shoot a sequence that will edit together neatly or don't know how to light a good interview or scene or get decent audio in a difficult location. And if you are under pressure to get the job done in a short amount of time then that's when mistakes happen.

The book gives you information about the tips and techniques that professional camera people use day in and day out in order to get consistently good video, and solve location problems, whatever camera they are using, and also get you to the next stage of shooting. It is a practical guide to video shooting and production.

Hopefully, it will make location shooting on video more enjoyable for you as well. After all if you're not enjoying yourself when shooting then when are you...

No matter what camera you use, from a palmcorder to HDCam-SR, this book will help you develop a practical, consistent way of working by identifying the important jobs and tasks to be done on location and concentrating on these. By simplifying the way you shoot and creating a routine you will get better results so that even the busiest of location shoots can go well and leave you confident that your rushes will be fine and make a great final cut. You'll learn how to solve many location shooting problems and also have some tricks up your sleeve to show you can add value and quality to any shoot. After all the camera is only the hardware, but you, the cameraperson, are the important part, you are the software that brings it to life...

From students to journalists shooting on SONY's HVR-Z1e (or simply the Z1 as it's becoming fondly known as) to camera assistants moving up, sound recordists, editors or production staff changing roles and people who want to improve their video location shooting techniques, better location shooting aims to increase your knowledge of the day-by-day tips and techniques needed to survive in today's shooting environment. Perhaps you are thinking of becoming a freelance cameraperson and want to find out more about how best to handle different and sometimes difficult location shoots, if so then I hope this book will give you many answers and some inspiration as well.

All the solutions are taken from professional people shooting in the real world who have worked out the hard way how best to solve video shooting problems on location.

About the Author

In the film and TV business your CV is your calling card and the best way I can introduce myself is by giving you a glance at my CV which stretches from 1972 to today. I started my career in TV at the age of 18 as a junior studio cameraman and have worked up through many grades since then, running two production companies on the way and have shot on most types of cameras, video and film,

NARRATION
"Shooting skidoos for GMTV on location with sound recordist Ian Birch."

all on location since the 1970s. I'm still a working cameraman and director today and spend 4 days a week shooting for the BBC at Westminster London on location shoots. I've put the CV at the end of this chapter, make of it what you will, hopefully it shows that I've done a fair bit of shooting and tackled a few challenges over the years, and you'll know me a bit better from having seen it.

Most of my adult life has been spent filming on location for TV programs, film commercials and corporate programs over a period of 26 years during which time I've shot on many formats, from 35 mm for cinema commercials, 16 mm for fashion, music and docs, Beta and DigiBeta for TV series, DVCAM for current affairs and corporate. During this period I've been lucky enough to also produce and direct many broadcast TV series and other commercial video projects and have run two production companies for this purpose.

But I actually started my TV career as a studio cameraman at ATV studios in London, where each camera trainee went through 1 year probation training period, to see if you were up to the mark and then a further 3 years of on-the-job experience before becoming a substantive cameraman. It's sounds old-fashioned now in an age where media colleges and university courses in TV seem to be the way to start a career, but back then in the 1970s, when cheesecloth shirts and loon pants were (mistakenly) regarded as great fashion items, this was the only way to get started in TV, film and video. This was a typical apprenticeship you would find many other industries. The joy of learning camera work this way was twofold, firstly you were actually being paid whilst you learnt, so you could buy more cheesecloth shirts and flared pants in strange colors, and secondly you could make all your mistakes in the apprenticeship period with experienced people around to help you sort them out. And because of this you were far more willing to take chances and try out different ideas. It was a good way to explore TV and find out how best to do your job without being overly worried about making career threatening mistakes.

My location filming work started when the new generation of lightweight portable cameras came along in the mid-1970s, although they still had an umbilical cable that needed to be attached to a portable VTR machine. For the first time you could simply pick up the video camera and shoot somewhere other than a studio. A simple step you might think, but back then it was revolutionary and would put TV cameramen on an equal footing as film cameramen whose 16 mm Arri's and Aaton's were widely used for location shooting.

These new video TV cameras would change the working lives of most video cameramen throughout the world.

Then came the breakthrough of the SONY Betacam which had the VTR included into its body and things changed once again for video cameramen. Using this kit I went on to film in most parts of the world and was then asked to direct and produce programs for U.K. TV stations, on location. These opportunities would never have come my way if the new cameras had not been introduced.

I have now filmed, directed and produced over 98 broadcast TV shows, most of which are location based. One lovely TV series called "Go Fishing" took me filming in India, Northwest territories of Canada, U.S.A., Kenya, Zimbabwe and most of Europe. Again it would not have been possible for a video cameraman to do this work without the new location style cameras; it would most certainly have gone to a film operator without this development.

Back in the 1980s it was difficult for a video cameraman to get jobs on film shoots, which were closely guarded by long-standing film crews who closed ranks on video people trying to shoot film. However with a bit of perseverance I managed to get a few small jobs on 16 mm shoots and learnt about lighting for film mainly through good hearted film lighting cameramen who patiently answered my barrage of questions on their lighting rigs and setups. Eventually after a lot of small film jobs, I was asked to shoot and light 35 mm productions and this again was a great period of learning about different techniques – how film stocks varied, how processing and colorizing can affect your lighting and how film editors worked.

I changed my way of working forever after this.

It was obvious from the film work that a shoot could go spectacularly wrong if the cameraman did not plan everything in advance and also find out exactly how the editor was going to edit the job. Some producers had very limited technical knowledge and would not explain properly how they were going to treat the film after shooting. The more planning I put into the pre-filming stages, the less chance there was of problems in the edit stage, and producers using the well-worn phrase "but I thought you knew we were going to do x, y and z for the final cut."

I now apply the same process to video shoots and pre-shooting I talk to everyone in the production chain and make copious notes about what they want and how the finished production will look. By doing this any conflicts between the filming stage and the editing style, look, content, amount of shots needed will be spotted before the camera has been taken out of the bag and everyone then has a good idea of what the rushes will contain before they are viewed.

Now we have cameras which are so small and light, with picture quality that is to die for and access to locations around the globe simply by jumping on a plane. So life for camera people and VJs must be easier than it has been 20 years ago? You can even put the camera on auto and it will be fine? Shooting is now simpler? The new cameras have ironed out many location filming problems.

Er not quite...

This is why I wanted to write a book which explained the best way to solve location filming problems and help beginners and intermediate camera people, VJ's, students, journalists and video enthusiasts learn the easiest way to better results.

Directed the successful pilot for OKTV! (ITV & Carlton). Created a series for Carlton. Worked on interactive and streamed video projects.

Worked for most of the major TV stations, and production companies; fast worker with a good reputation. Can edit on AVID and FCP.

CHAPTER 1

Location Filming Equipment

The choice of equipment available today for location filming is simply huge, ranging from small prosumer units capable of HDV (high definition video) and AVCHD (advanced codec high definition, capable of storing full HD, and 1920 × 1080 resolution onto memory cards and hard disk drives). Then through to SONY's DigiBetacams, XDCAM with its HD resolution and hard disk storage, Panasonic P2, up to top ranging HDCAM-SR cameras with 14-bit multiframe rate and either 4:4:4 or 4:2:2 output rates. Whether you are in the market to purchase a kit or are hiring on a regular basis, you can spend many, many hours looking at different cameras and audio gear and then comparing specifications, prices, weights, etc. Reaching a decision on what is best for you and whether this choice will then retain its value and usefulness over the coming years is a major job in itself and very time consuming.

In this chapter, I'll help you define some basics about video kits that will help narrow down how you make that choice. As far as possible we'll categorize types of cameras and kits and highlight the types of shooting they are best at, so that the choice is again made a bit easier. We'll be looking at the types of cameras from a camera operator's point of view to see what benefits each camera brings to everyday working.

It's impossible to list all video cameras in this book as new ones will soon be out in the marketplace, but the ones here are used consistently and probably will be for a long time to come, and therefore there is a good chance that we will be either buying them or hiring them at some point of time.

FIG 1.1
SONY HVR-Z1e, Ikegami HL-DV7w, SONY DSR 450WSPL pack shot. "Location video cameras, big and small. SONY HVR-Z1e, Ikegami HL-DV7w DVCAM plus SONY's DVCAM the DSR 450WSPL."

In Chapter 6, we'll talk about standardizing the way you work with any and every camera from the humblest palmcorder to mighty ENG kits (Figure 1.2) and the point of this is to prove that it's not the camera that matters so much but the operator and that you will work faster making less mistakes with this process in mind. Armed with this knowledge you'll be able to pick up any new kit that's just appeared and soon be able to film as confidently with it as you were with your old kit.

If you work for a TV station or any large production company, then there is a good chance that your kit has been provided for you, possibly without your input. If this is so then jump ahead to the sections about the kit that is relevant to you. If you are freelance or take contract work, then it's crucial that your kit suits the video work you intend to do and has a good shelf life; you don't want to be repurchasing after a short period if your kit doesn't do the job correctly or it records in a format that is to be replaced in the near future.

If you hire or use other people's kits, then it will be important for you to know the fundamentals about each individual camera and how the important functions are located and accessed, and this will make your life easier when you come to use them.

If you are in the process of choosing a new camera system, then the following list may help you decide the priorities that will affect your purchase. There are so

FIG 1.2
Cameraman at 10 Downing Street. "Location shooting comes in all forms, here its news and current affairs in London."

many decisions to be made before buying a new location shooting kit that it's worthwhile trying to look objectively at the main points that matter. It applies to most types and levels of video cameras from semi-pro up to full blown HD:

- Firstly and most importantly you need to check out the post-shooting workflow taking you all the way from video gathering and editing to graphics and sound dubbing (if you use this facility). There are now multiple systems and ways to take in camera rushes, edit, and then package the final cut that it will almost always affect the camera and format you shoot on. The main point here is that you don't want to end up with a shooting kit that makes the editing long and difficult. So check and recheck that the format you are choosing has a smooth, sensible progress through editing, and don't choose a format on the basis that "it will soon be supported with edit software." Go for a tried and tested route and ask the retailers hard direct questions about the level of support for that format.
- What tape/disk format does the camera kit use? Can your existing decks and software handle it?
- Will your existing clients be happy to use this camera format or do they only want to work with their existing decks and formats?

- Will the rushes digitize/transfer quickly and efficiently with your existing edit software?
- Will you need to buy new lenses or can your existing lenses be used on the new camera? Can it accept third party lenses from pro makers such as Canon and Fujinon?
- Check any lens coming with a new camera to see what maximum aperture it works at. Does this stated aperture change when the lens zooms into its tight end? If it does alter aperture (ramping down) then decide if this will affect your day-by-day shooting as a few less stop of light could mean you end up having to use extra lighting on your locations.
- What batteries will it take and can you use an existing battery system or will new ones be needed? A new battery system always seems to work out as an expensive option after you've bought new chargers and a few battery units.
- What audio capabilities does the new unit have, how many tracks, what bit rate, and are the connectors industry standard? Will your existing audio gear work correctly with this kit?
- What digital compression does the camera provide for its tapes? DigiBetacam is a mild 2:1 compression, whereas all DVCAMs are 5:1. Getting technical for a brief instance it's worth noting that the DV system uses a different compression system than DigiBetacam, which is more efficient. As DV editing is now very common, DigiBetacam tapes are often compressed to DV for postproduction work. HD compression takes its starting point from the DV system, which is a modern technique.
- And then you'll have to look at the camera's performance: Is it 3 CCDs? What size are they? Larger sensors mean less noise. How does it handle its luminance, chrominance, and color signals, and what sampling ration is used?

Sampling is the description of how many times each second a signal is looked at. A DV camera will sample the Y (luminance part of the signal or brightness) at 13.5 MHz (13.5 million times per second). It then compares this to the other two main video components, R − Y (red minus the luminance) and B − Y (blue minus the luminance) and expresses it as a ratio. While DV is 4:2:0 in PAL (Phase Alternating Line) or 4:1:1 in NTSC (National Television System Committee), DigiBeta is 4:2:2.

However Panasonic DVC Pro is 4:1:1 and is DV compression, and DVC Pro 50 and Pro 100 are also DV compressions and used on HD cameras.

A very good description of sampling and how it can be compared can be found in Jon Fauer's Focal Press book *Shooting Digital Video*. This book is not overly technical and you can quickly see how the whole system works.

So let's take a look at the smaller kits first.

The latest generation of prosumer/semi-pro cameras such as SONY HVR-Z1e, Canon XL-H1, and JVC 251 all offer versions of high definition video known as HDV. This was a joint development by SONY, Canon, JVC, and Sharp and was introduced in 2003. Its basic purpose is to take the line resolutions of HD at 1080i or 720p and encode them onto DV tape. SONY used the 1080i, whereas others used 720p. Canon also uses 1080i and Panasonic can shoot both (full HD for TV is 1920 × 1080). These cameras are smaller than a full blown ENG camera, such as a SONY DVCAM DSR 570 or 450, and if you believe the manufacturers' marketing releases, they will do everything perfectly well for 100.1% of the time.

So that's sorted out then…

These are the kits that TV companies are giving out to staff in order to shoot their own shows, packages, and clips. These are also being used for mainstream TV more and more, and in their own way they are fantastic tools. But they are not ideal for every type of shooting, as they will not perform as perfectly as ENG cameras (electronic newsgathering cameras is a generic term for the larger, portable cameras that you see shooting TV news, sport, and features material). These are of broadcast quality, with high picture resolution, many manual functions, separate lenses, plus a high price tag. And at times the smaller video cameras will simply make your working life harder. The key is to find out as much about the kit and what it can/can't do before using it and avoid being tempted by endless menu functions that are not going to help you or functions that only have a limited benefit on your day's work. It must be relevant and useful and not just a gimmick.

In these new prosumer cameras, many functions are hidden in the camera's menu systems making them slow to access and increasing the chance of having the wrong function switched on in a menu somewhere and the operator not being aware of it. Other major functions such as aperture control are sometimes in strange positions, not where you expect them to be, and work slightly differently than the ENG kits. The original SONY HVR-Z1e has a small silver aperture wheel mounted on the front of the camera's body, which is awkward if you want to adjust it quickly while shooting, and you can easily go the wrong way, stopping the camera down when you meant to open it up and vice versa (Figures 1.3 and 1.4).

FIG 1.3
SONY Z1 camera. "Sony HVR-Z1e".

FIG 1.4
SONY Z1 aperture wheel close-up. "Someone at SONY decided to put the aperture ring down here…why I wonder?"

Why didn't they leave the aperture ring on the lens, where every camera person in the world has been used to finding it and where it works best? If a car manufacturer decided to put the steering wheel in the back seats, everyone would be totally bewildered. I want my steering wheel in front of the driver's seat please, and as a cameraman the aperture control back on the lens…

Audio outputs and inputs on these prosumer cameras are now starting to be XLR as standard instead of phonos, which are much better and easier to use as the XLR is balanced and most mics accept XLR leads and which makes adding extension cables easy as well (Figure 1.5). Another good point from a location point of view is that the XLR connectors are tough and will withstand a lot of hard work compared to the smaller phono setup. And if you

TIP

SONY HVR-Z1e...When filming in standard definition, the viewfinder does not show the whole frame, and therefore when you play back the tape on another source machine, things like microphones and other items that you thought were out of frame while shooting have suddenly appeared in the shot. In HDV mode this doesn't happen: what you see is what you get. Some people film in HDV and then down convert back to DV so they are not bothered by this annoying problem...Beware.

FIG 1.5
"Inputs for proper audio… XLRs on the SONY HVR-Z1e."

are out shooting with other crews around you and your mic leads break down, someone is bound to have an XLR lead handy to lend you.

I'm not being negative about this breed of camera, just realistic. The final picture quality is very good indeed and they are small and easily transported, you just have to be aware of their limitations when it comes to different types of shooting. For instance you would not want to use a SONY HVR-Z1e or Canon XL-H1 on a sports event where long lens filming is needed. But if you need to shoot interviews and stand-ups for inserting into your program then they would be fine, as long as you know how to use them and how to access the different menu items quickly.

So let's look at what cameras are best for different types of shoots.

What we'll try and do is highlight how well each category of camera can cope with different types of shooting and from that you'll be able to make a better judgment of the usefulness of the individual kits for the filming you do.

The smaller cameras are normally quite lightweight, which is good if you are traveling, or working on your own and have to carry their kit around with you. But this means they will not be as robust as full-blown ENG cameras over many years of hard usage. Shooting documentaries, interviews, pieces to camera, second camera or B roll, music, and travel productions on location with these cameras can work well but you have to take care with fundamental items like focus, aperture, and audio.

The reason I say this is that many people still use these cameras on full auto setting as standard and you can find problems such as nonaccurate focussing. A subject in front of the lens can appear to be out of focus compared to the background, which seems to be more in focus. Audio left totally on auto can have mismatched levels, and gain can be higher than normal if left on auto. Many video editors complain that these are some of the most common mistakes they see from people shooting with these smaller kits.

As far as focus goes this softness of the subject can also occur even when the camera's are being used in manual as the circuitry works in a distinct way. The camera's filtering system sees a hard edged background, which is static, and compares it to the foreground subject, which will have some movement, and while processing the image the background appears to the viewer as somewhat sharper. So if, for instance, you are shooting an interview and also asking the questions, then having got your subject framed up, you can easily miss the fact

that the background is sharper than the subject: easy to do, especially when using the LCD screen in daylight and trying to concentrate on two things at once. But as long as you know that this can occur you can check for it and also set up the shot so that the background is slightly out of focus compared to the foreground by using a longer lens and a wider aperture, or maintain more distance between the camera and the subject. If you are not aware of this then you probably won't know anything is wrong until you sit down and view the tapes for editing; too late to do anything about it then.

But if you are shooting high end interviews, say celebrities or opening pieces to camera for an important production, then you are better off using the capabilities of a larger ENG camera simply because you have so much more control over the way the camera can be used. As always in life it falls into patterns, and many people now use the smaller cameras to shoot insert shots, clips, and cutaway on a show while using the larger cameras for the main stuff. Partly because of its cost efficient budgeting, you'll get two hire days of SONY HVR-Z1e costs compared to one of a DVcam/ENG camera and crew, and partly it allows a production company to keep more control over its productions by having a camera in-house and then being able to use it as and when it wants.

Now becoming more common for shooting is Panasonic's P2 solid state recording camera system with removable cards instead of tape and SONY's Z7, which uses interchangeable lenses as standard and allows tape or flash disk recording. The move to solid state recording and HD format is well on the way.

LENSES AND CHIPS

Small cameras will normally have an integral lens that cannot be changed, and therefore you will be stuck with this one lens. Canon's XL 1 range does have changeable zooms and like all Canon optics these are very good. Many of these cameras will accept a wide-angle adapter to slip over the existing lens, useful if you want to film in cramped rooms. The real difference between larger video cameras and the smaller ones lies in the size and the speed of the light collecting devices used by each one. Many cameras use CCDs, charged couple devices, as their chip or sensor system, which are highly sensitive to light. Pro ENG location video cameras will use 2/3 in. chips, and smaller cameras such as the SONY HVR-Z1e or Canon XL-H1 use 1/3 in. devices. HDV cameras are starting to use complimentary metal oxide semiconductor (CMOS) chips as their collection system, which can reduce noise, and are cheaper to produce than normal CCDs.

The smaller the chip, the harder it is to achieve a shallow depth of focus, which is where the item you have focussed on stands out from the items behind and in front of it. The smaller chips have a tendency to create a deeper depth of field, which is where all the items in the frame look sharp, not just the one you have focussed on. These chips also have different sensitivities to light that acts like the ASA rating of film, and that again affects the look of your final shots. When you look at the specifications of your camera, you'll see different ways of expressing this sensitivity, sometimes as Lux, and this will affect how much light you will need to put on your subject when shooting it.

The chip size also affects the lens' field of view as well. Another benefit of the larger chip size is that there is less noise in the final picture.

If you go the route of using a wide angle adaptor then purchase one that allows you to zoom through it as well because some of them don't let you do this. Likewise you can get adapters to extend the tight end of the lens if needed (Figure 1.6).

FIG 1.6

"Century Optics wide-angle adapter. You can zoom through this version which will increase the angle of view by .7. This is also available in .6 and .8 versions. SONY makes a version as well but it does not allow zooming through."

Look at the lens to find out the widest f-stop it works at. Some cameras with integral zooms stop down (work at a smaller aperture) as you zoom in, which will mean extra lighting in some interior locations. Also check the ratio of the optical zoom. 5:1, 10:1, or more gives you a good working range. Find out if the zoom servo (the rocker button that operates the zoom) works at a reasonable speed and allows you to start and stop the zoom smoothly and without any snatchy movements. If the movement seems too rough or coarse, then this will show on your shots and make very untidy zooms in and out. You will notice the jumpy movement in the viewfinder as you depress the zoom rocker button. There's no point in looking at the digital part of the zoom spec, which starts after the lens optics have zoomed in to the tightest part of its optical length, as the final picture quality will suffer from picture noise if you get into this part of the lens, and all lenses should have a smooth action on the focus ring.

The integral lens is not a drawback for many types of shooting but if you want to film on long lenses, say sports or wildlife filming, then it will be a problem if you can't get in tight enough on your subjects. And if you are continually screwing on adapters for some shots and taking them off for others then this will hinder your work as well.

For example the lens on a SONY HVR-Z1e has a zoom range of 4.5–45 mm, which in real-world terms means that if you want to shoot a mid-shot of a subject the farthest distance from the camera you can do this is approximately 10 m. After this you have run out of zoom range. So unless you know this, and if it proves a problem for the work you normally shoot, then a longer length lens might suit you better.

In comparison most ENG kits allow you to choose a separate zoom from other manufacturers such as Canon or Fujinon and will accept these without any problem (Figure 1.7). So you can use a lens that complements your filming. You will have to pay a premium for this but the quality, durability, and usefulness of these lenses will be better than most integral lenses.

These lenses offer ranges from 11-1 to 40-1 and f-stops that are wide enough to shoot in very low light. The 40-1 Canon HJ40 × 14 IASD has an inbuilt image stabilizer with a wide angle of 34.9 degrees and will remove 50,000 earth pounds or 57,420 earth dollars from your wallet when you say "I'll take it"... The wide angle of Canon's J11 × 4.5 lens is a massive 88 degrees with a 2× extender built in so you get the benefit of working with a lovely wide angle and also having the extender to shoot tighter shots when needed, an added benefit for location shooting.

FIG 1.7
"A standard ENG lens made by Canon. 18× zoom and a 9 mm wide end with a two times extender as well. Labeled as 'IF' it will focus using internal lens elements rather than external ones. Strong enough to withstand years of shooting in even the roughest locations and with good optics."

Many other ENG zooms also have the option of a 2× extender that you simply switch in and get the benefit of added focal length to your optics, and you need to open the exposure one or two stops when this extender or "doubler" is in position.

These third party lenses have a focus ring with definite end stops at each end, so you can tell when you are on infinity (far distance) or the near (close) end. The benefit of this is that you always know where you are focussed. Some prosumer cameras have a focus adjustment with no end stops, and you can get confused about where the lens is actually focussed. Whether it is on the foreground, mid-area, or in the background you will notice that in very bright, contrasty lighting conditions it becomes difficult to see where the camera is focussed as it will be working at such a small aperture which creates the effect of deep focus and it can be hard to judge the correct focus position on the small LCD screens that cameras now use. What a mistake they can be…

A Canon or Fujinon location ENG lens is a very well-made unit, therefore always choose this option if you want quality and long life from your lens. No doubt you'll pay more but all the positive points and longer life will soon override this.

HD cameras, such as SONY's ranging from HDCAM, XDCAM, and up to HDCAM-SR, etc., are meant to be used with HD lenses again supplied by makers such as Canon. I know some location cameramen who still use their standard definition (SD) lenses on their HD units for most day-to-day work and then when they get

an important HD shoot they hire in the HD lenses as needed. As the camera facilities house over the world start buying in HD cameras, they are also stocking the HD lenses and not just the SD ones. As long as you check to make sure that your SD camera can physically accept an HD lens, these can be used.

TRIPODS

I'm always surprised at how some retailers try and sell unsuitable tripods to people wanting to buy video equipment just because they are going to use them on prosumer video kits. Just because you choose to film with a smaller camera unit than, say, a full blown ENG camera doesn't mean that you will accept a cheaper option for a tripod. In fact a lighter camera means that the tripod head has to do more work in order to keep pans and tilts smooth and glitch free. The heavier cameras with large batteries provide a solid mass that helps the tripod head to move efficiently, whereas a lighter camera reduces this mass and the tripod head has more work to do in order to keep the pan and tilt movements consistent.

Fluid heads with efficient pan and tilt braking and an adjustable balance to allow for different camera weights, batteries, etc. are the way to go with any size video camera. And any camera moves that you attempt on the tight end of your zoom will visibly benefit from a good quality head and legs.

It goes without saying that the tripod has to be sturdy enough for the camera you are using but makers like Vinten and Sachtler have precise guides to their tripods and heads stating which cameras are suitable for them. Miller tripods provide an alternative to the big two above as well (Figures 1.8–1.11).

Avoid tripods that are for stills cameras and general photographic work. These are quite inadequate for video work and you will never quite trust the head when you want to do a nice camera move. They are primarily designed to keep a stills camera stationery, so no movement occurs when the shutter is pressed. This normally means that very little design has gone into the head when it comes to panning and tilting, and if you can't do these two things smoothly and precisely then your video work will suffer and you'll be making excuses to keep your subject static in the frame without any movement being included. Look for balance adjustments so that if you change from a lightweight battery to a heavy duty one, then the camera and the new battery can be adjusted forward to compensate for the change in weight. Video camera heads should be capable of smooth movement that is not coarse or uneven even when the camera is on its longest lens. If your tripod doesn't provide all these, then it's time to trade up.

FIG 1.8
Sachtler ENG tripod. "This Sachtler 18P copes well with most ENG cameras."

FIG 1.9
SONY Z1 tripod Sachtler 14P. "This Sachtler 14p head and legs is designed for smaller semi-pro cameras but allow you to do smooth pans and tilts as well, unlike many photographic tripods."

FIG 1.10
"Proper adjusters for pan and tilt, balance and a spirit level will allow you to make smooth clean moves on shot time after time."

FIG 1.11
"And the legs have a simple but effective, single lever clasp to allow height adjustment."

For location work your tripod needs to be a combination of good performance when shooting, robust enough to take the knocks from traveling and constant rigging and not too heavy.

There is a very good reason for getting as good a tripod as you can afford for location shooting. Later in the book we go into the importance of filming a good variety of shots for the final edit and how important this is for the video editor as well as for giving the end production a high standard of visual interest. And if you are shooting in a great location you'll want to get the best out of it, which means lots of wide shots and lots of tight shots on the end of the lens to make for an interesting mix of frame sizes for the final cut. If your tripod and head aren't good enough to give you smooth pans and tilts on the end of the zoom then you will rapidly become fed up with this and stick to safer, wider shots, and as a result your rushes will all become very similar with little visual variation in them.

So whereas it might seem that there is no direct link from a tripod to a good looking end show, you can now see that this is not the case and that there is a relationship from one to the other… (Figure 1.12).

Finally it pays to buy a good strong but lightweight tripod case at the same time you purchase the tripod, and if you plan to fly with the kit make sure the case can withstand the rigors of airport baggage handling.

FIG 1.12
"JVC 251 video camera. Lighter than a normal ENG kit but still needs a good head and legs to let the best performance from it."

POWER SOURCES

Other benefits of the prosumer kits include small, lightweight batteries giving many hours of camera usage under normal conditions. Lithium ion technology has transformed battery performance. By comparison the well-established ENG kits are heavier and take larger batteries. A number of battery systems are made for these kits from PAG, SONY, Anton-Bauer, etc. and you simply have to choose the system that you prefer. Cost for every component will be more than the smaller cameras, which is a drawback if you are on a tight budget. However with this added cost you will get a better made unit with a long life capable of taking rough working in the outside world, although not everyone wants to commit to the cost for these pro kits.

Popular pro video camera kits at the moment are SONY Beta SP in the U.S., SONY DSR 570/450 DVCAMs in the U.K., and DigiBetacam to a lesser extent these days, although the pictures it produces remain superb thanks to its mild 2-1 compression.

Finally some cameras now have clever ways of telling you how much power is left on your battery. For instance the SONY DSR 570/450 allows you to go into the menu and tell the camera that types of batteries you intend to power it

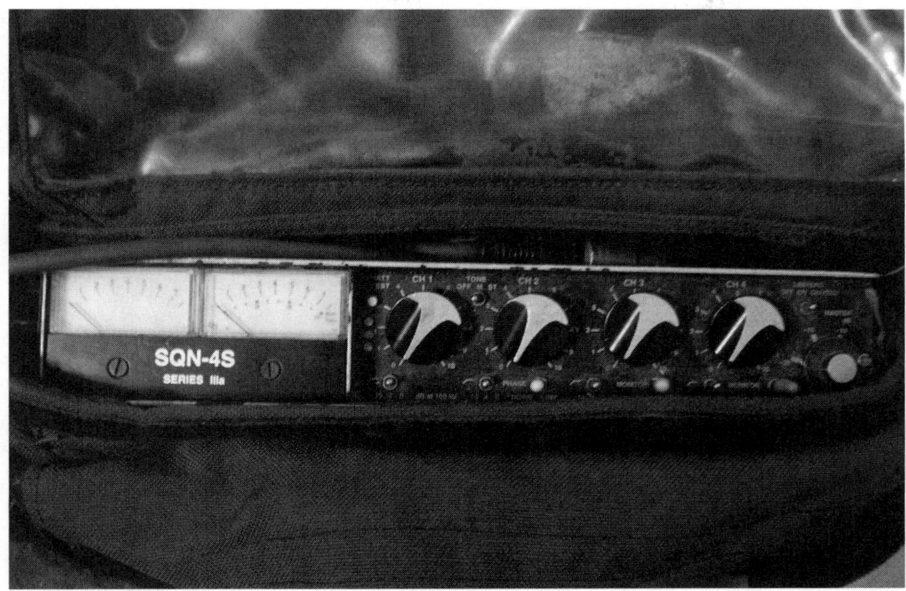

FIG 1.13
SQN mixer. "SQN mixers are used in many countries of the world and again they are strong enough to withstand the rigors of location shooting in any country."

with. The camera will then align its battery readings on the rear LCD screen to show the correct power falloff for the chosen battery.

The logic behind this being that some types of batteries will have a different falloff rate than others. For example if you use PAG batteries you have a choice of the original large type or the newer, smaller block versions, which now come with a power meter on the rear. However if you use these small batteries and rely on the cameras power display on the LCD screen to tell you how much life is left in the battery, then you'll get a shock because these batteries can cut out with very little warning. The larger versions tail off gently and you can see this on the camera readout. So don't get caught out.

AUDIO

Audio capabilities on the smaller cameras vary but as discussed above look for inputs on the camera that are XLRs and will then accept pro mics and leads. You will also want to be able to switch from the onboard camera mic to plug in personals/clip mics and handheld ones like Sennheiser 416's without going deep into menus and submenus. Likewise if you want to be able to alter the mic's levels easily, try and avoid cameras that only allow you access to this in menus. Switches, meters, and dials on the outside of the camera are always better for instant audio adjustments. However the very best way to gather good audio from one or more microphones on location is by use of a sound mixer (Figure 1.13).

The choice of how many audio tracks needed depends on the work you do, but a minimum of two tracks is necessary for most video work. This way you can at least split the audio from two subjects and alter the levels individually. This then allows you to alter each track separately when the rushes are fed into the edit machine and allows for neater audio editing.

TIP

Personal microphones can suffer from terrible wind noise in blustery conditions as they have such a small sized head. All you hear is popping and whining due to the wind blustering around the mic head and the subject's voice fights to be heard over this din, so grab some little wind gags that push on over the mic's head. Because these are a simple push-on fit they can get dropped and lost at a frightening rate, so use a small drop of superglue when you put them on and you'll save yourself many pounds over the years.

Although you don't really need these gags on when shooting indoors, the sound quality won't be compromised by them being on permanently, so it's a worthwhile exercise to do. They cost about £10 ($18) each to replace...

Generally the audio kit for both types of cameras is fairly similar and will depend on whether you shoot as a one-man band or if you work with a sound recordist. One-man bands will need a handheld mic capable of plugging into the camera, a couple of personals like SONY's ECM 77's, or similar for two-handed interviews, and some XLR extension cables and a radio mic for cable free work (Figure 1.14). There is much more information on location audio equipment in Chapter 5.

The above audio items will allow you to cover most location shoots, and if you get more complicated setups then its best using a sound recordist anyway.

A sound mixer will allow you to take in and balance multiple microphones and then feed out a balanced, mixed level to the camera's two audio inputs. This is immensely useful if you are filming lots of people on a set or need to use a mixture of different mics. Industry standard audio mixers for location work used by sound recordists all over the world are made by SQN, sound developments, and sound devices.

OTHER POINTS TO CONSIDER

White balance and gain switches should be easy to access and preferably on the camera body, and not in menus. Shutter adjustments can be used to get rid of

the roll bar that sometimes appears in the viewfinder when you shoot a screen with a refresh rate different to your camera. See Figure 1.15 for more information about these and other fundamental controls.

FIG 1.14
ENG one-man band sound kit. "My own sound kit suitable for one-man band shooting has essentials, such as ECM 77 tie mics, small handheld mic powered from the camera and various XLR audio leads. I also use a Sennheiser handheld radio mic which is good for press conferences as it can be put into a small desktop holder and left at the lectern and podium."

FIG 1.15
Viewfinder brightness/ contrast, and peaking pots. "Essential controls should always be physically accessible on your video camera and not tucked away in a menu somewhere. These are standard adjusters found on a DigiBetacam."

TIP

If the camera shutter cannot get rid of this roll bar and you are filming a computer screen try changing the screen rate in the computer. You normally find this adjustment in the control panel menu. LCD screens don't suffer from this problem.

Also make sure that the camera has manual settings for focus, aperture, white balance, gain, and shutter, with easy access also to brightness, contrast, and peaking controls, which according to me should always be physical adjustments and never menu items.

OTHER SUPPORTS AND MOUNTS

The manufacturers would have us believe that the smaller cameras are great for handheld use. Well to a point that's true, but if you want to shoot with the camera on your shoulder for any length of time, say a fashion show or pop concert, then they have serious drawbacks. Many smaller camera shapes are simply not comfortable enough to use for any length of time either handheld or shoulder mounted. Even though they weigh less than ENG kits you will find that when you have to support them in your hand for any length of time it becomes uncomfortable, and your shots will suffer as your arm gets tired.

TIP

SONY's popular HVR-Z1e can link the gain to the iris, and if you are in manual mode, you find that it keeps altering the gain whenever you alter the iris. You need to disable this to make them work separately.

The ENG type of camera is undoubtedly heavier but should balance correctly on your shoulder leaving you free to film, without worrying about the camera falling off or tipping forward or backward. You'll also be able to access the zoom and focus rings without taking your hands away from their holding position, which you can't do on some prosumer kits.

So if you do want to shoot a fair amount of handheld video with your smaller camera, it's worthwhile looking at some third party mounts that help this. I've seen a round mount called the "Fig-Rig" in which you mount a smaller video camera in the middle and then use the ring to hold and control it (Figure 1.16). Always have a long test/play of any equipment like this before parting with your hard earned bucks as they suit some people but not everyone.

FIG 1.16
"The Fig-Rig... designed to give easier handling for smaller video cameras."

STEADICAM

Steadicams now play an important part in location shooting and are increasingly common on every type of video and TV shoot (Figure 1.17). You can see them used on football and rugby matches with the operators running up and down the sidelines following the action in close shots and with silky smooth movements. Before the advent of steadicam in the early 1970s by American Garrett Brown, the handheld cameraman doing this shot simply had to put the camera on his shoulder, bend his knees slightly, tie the camera cable to his belt, and then run at a sideways angle, like a crab, and hope for the best. The guys who were good at this seemed to have elastic bands for legs and a second set of eyes positioned just by their ears; they did well but if you showed their footage today in a split frame with a steadicam doing the same shot then I guess it would look a bit rough in comparison. And like the camera kit the steadicam units have steadily evolved, getting lighter and a more fluid movement to them.

There is a range of steadicams for most cameras and the first step is to choose the best system for your kit, firstly going by weight. Another make of camera stability mount for location use is Glidecam, who again offers units for different types of video and film cameras. Most steadicam units make use of three fundamental components – the post or sled where the camera, batteries, and monitor are mounted; the arm that has separate sections and springs and

FIG 1.17
Steadicam in action. "Steadicams are now a common part of TV and video productions and can support a wide range of cameras from 35 mm film to HVR-Z1e's."

allows the camera to "float"; and the vest, which the operator wears and which allows the weight of the entire unit to be carried evenly on his body.

At the top end a unit like the GPI Pro system, by George Paddock, is used in both the U.S. and the U.K. for cameras weighing between 10 and 55 lb (4.5 and 25 kg), so it will accept SONY DigiBetacams, HD cams, and also Arri film cameras.

Lighter cameras such as the SONY DSR 450/570 DVCAMs and HD cameras the 750 and 900 can use the steadicam Clipper 2, which takes weights from 10–50 lb (4.5–23 kgs). A lighter unit, which will handle the same cameras, is the Steadicam Archer (Figure 1.18).

And for SONY PD150/70 or HVR-Z1e, the Steadicam Flyer will handle weights from 5 to 15 lb (2.25–6.8 kg). It works in the same way as the full size systems do (Figure 1.19).

You can also now purchase a junior steadicam for smaller cameras, which gives you a consistently steady shot as you walk with your subject. We've used a few different types of these and it all seems to come down to how the camera is set up and balanced as to the results you get out of it. Some rigs are complicated to mount the camera on and it is infuriating when you try to balance the

FIG 1.18
Steadicam Archer. "The Steadicam Archer will support SONY DSR 450/570's and similar cameras up to 13.6 kg (30 lb)."

FIG 1.19
Steadicam Flyer. "Steadicam for the junior set? The Flyer can do the same smooth, fluid moves as its bigger brothers but using smaller cameras. A good bet if you are not an experienced steadicam operator."

camera before moving off to shoot. In fact one rig took four of us half a day to get going and even after that it was still hard to keep the camera balanced. So my advice is to go for one that has a straightforward setup procedure; otherwise it might spend most of its life in the box it came in holding your office door open. No matter what type of steadicam you use it should be capable of giving three main elements to the move/shot:

1. A steady or static opening shot holding on the subject for as long as is needed without any sign of movement, wobble, or flutter.
2. Smooth, floating moves keeping the camera balanced no matter where the arm is, high or low, and at the needed speed for the shot you are doing.
3. A final end shot that again can be held static without noticeable movement from the camera.

FIG 1.20
Z1 on Merlin steadicam rig. "Another option for smaller video cameras is the Merlin. It relies on getting the camera setup and is balanced perfectly on the mount. Any slight imbalance stops the unit from performing properly and you will be fighting the camera as it tips away from you. If you are using it for the first time, get the hire company to set it up for you with the camera you will be using loaded with the battery and tape as well. This will save a lot of time on location."

POLECAM

Polecam is a portable, lightweight solution to getting high, moving shots without resorting to expensive camera cranes, grips, and dollies (Figure 1.22). Its main advantages are the SD and HD signals it produces that can cut in well with other studio and outside broadcast cameras, ease of using it, and it is light to transport. This means that it can be more effective on shoots, and if you know how to use it correctly then it can add quite a lot of new production values to even simple jobs. It's formed from four to five carbon fiber sections

FIG 1.21
Easy rig with operator. "Another take on steadicam shots. The easy rig allows you to carry the weight of the camera on your back rather than on your shoulders. As it is supported from above and balanced, you can shoot tracking shots with a floating movement and the theory is that you can shoot for longer as the camera weight is spread over your body and not isolated on your shoulder alone."

of just over 1 m each in length and 4 cm in diameter (Figure 1.23). A counter-weight at one end and mini camera at the other are all balanced on a tripod or on a harness worn by the operator, and the whole kit can be put together within half an hour. A standard lens of 4 mm will give a 60 degree wide angle, useful for many shots (Figure 1.24). For location shooting it can be packed into two cases, and the camera head unit weighs a minimal 0.5 kg (1 lb).

You can view the shots by using an LCD monitor mounted on the boom and can operate the zoom by a joystick that works a small motor on the camera lens.

FIG 1.22
Polecam in operation on location. "Cheaper than a crane, portable and transportable in two bags, Polecam helps out on a location shoot."

Camera-wise it uses a Toshiba TU-63, which has 1/3rd sized sensors (or TU-62 1/2 sized sensors) mini camera with 3 chips and 750 lines of resolution, and the signal can be recorded onto a tape or fed by microwave link. There's also an optional SDI converter as well. Other mini-cams can also be used if you want to. Now that HDV and HD are becoming commonplace they have developed a separate camera head which will work with DVCAM and HDV cameras, and new small units like the SONY HC1, HC3, and HC5 video camcorders can be used with Polecam too. There is also an HD zoom lens made by Toshiba that can be used with their cameras (Figure 1.25).

I used Polecam for the title sequence on a TV series called "Fishing on the Edge", which was all about sea fishing in hard to get to places. The kit worked well but the only drawback we had was outdoor shooting in the awful January weather of the U.K. We were right by the shore, which had a stiff breeze hitting it for most of the day. The camera would start low and with a great wide shot and crane around and down in order to follow our presenter as he clambered over the slippy rocks then cast out into the waves, ending on a tight shot of his face.

Polecam worked well on the move but as it got to the final, tighter shot, the wind affected it and the camera head would not hold still. Its light weight proved a problem with stability and prevented it from being steady. As a result,

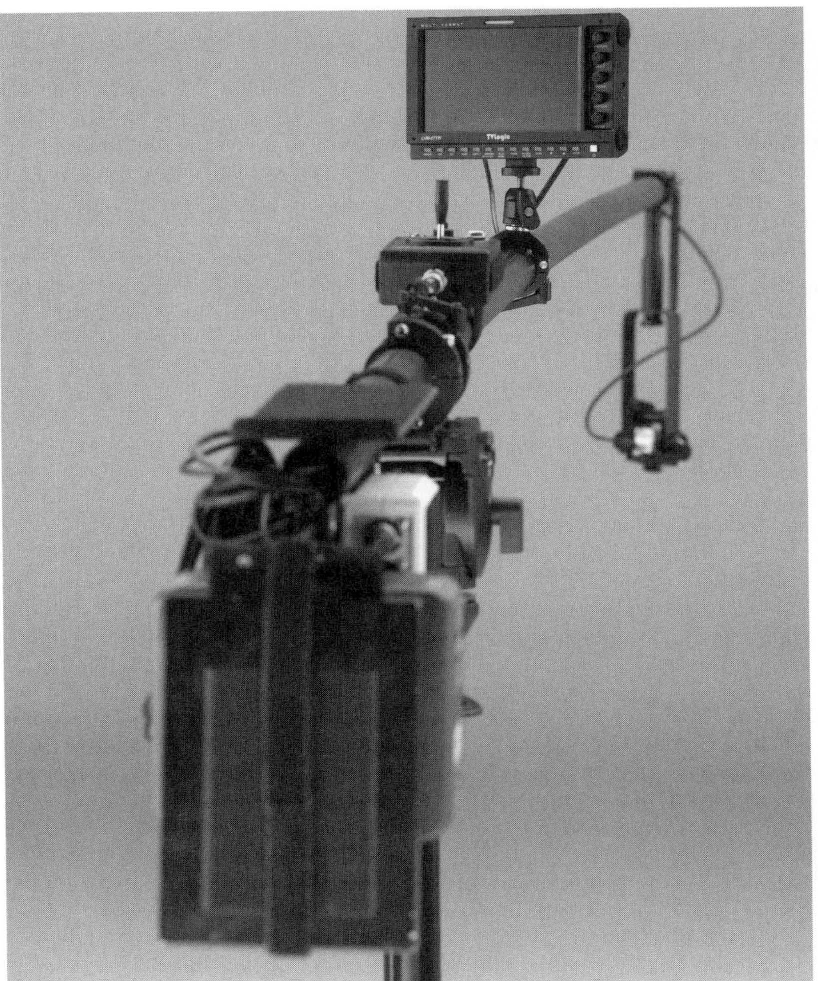

FIG 1.23
Polecam on tripod. "Polecam mounted on a tripod with the monitor and joystick for control of the zoom on the camera head."

there was a noticeable shaking in the camera, and the sequence needed a good 10–15 seconds of this end static shot to make it work. However, overall, the move worked so well that we decided to wait for the wind to ease off rather than compromise the sequence as it was the only shot we were recording that day, and eventually the shot worked perfectly. But it's a point to be aware of. You can't expect your camera support system to work in all weathers and every type of condition and in this case Polecam's low weight was the reason we were able to get to our isolated and remote location in the first place. No other crane or support system would have worked so well.

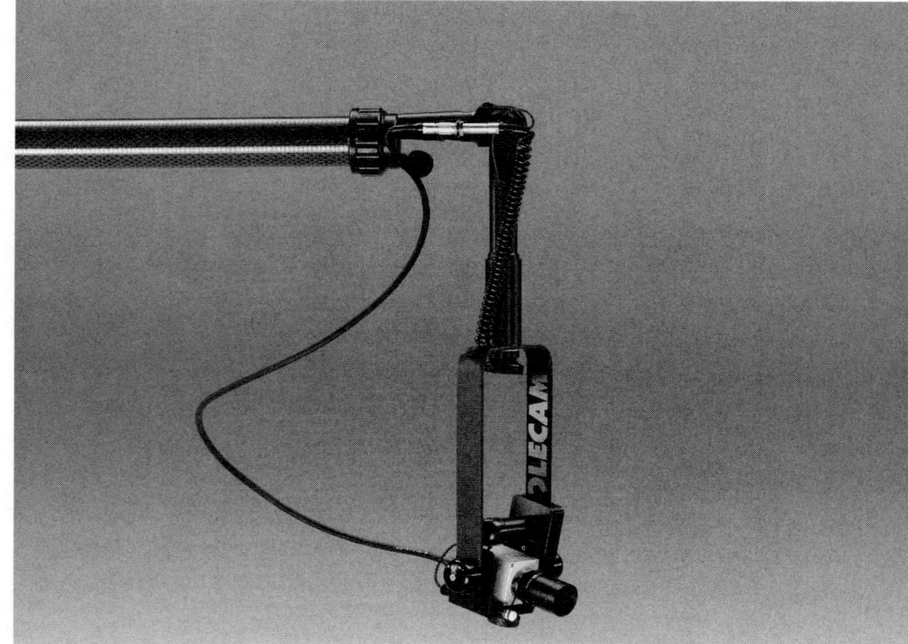

FIG 1.24
Polecam head.
"Down at the business end, the Toshiba camera sits in the camera head with all controls accessed back with the operator."

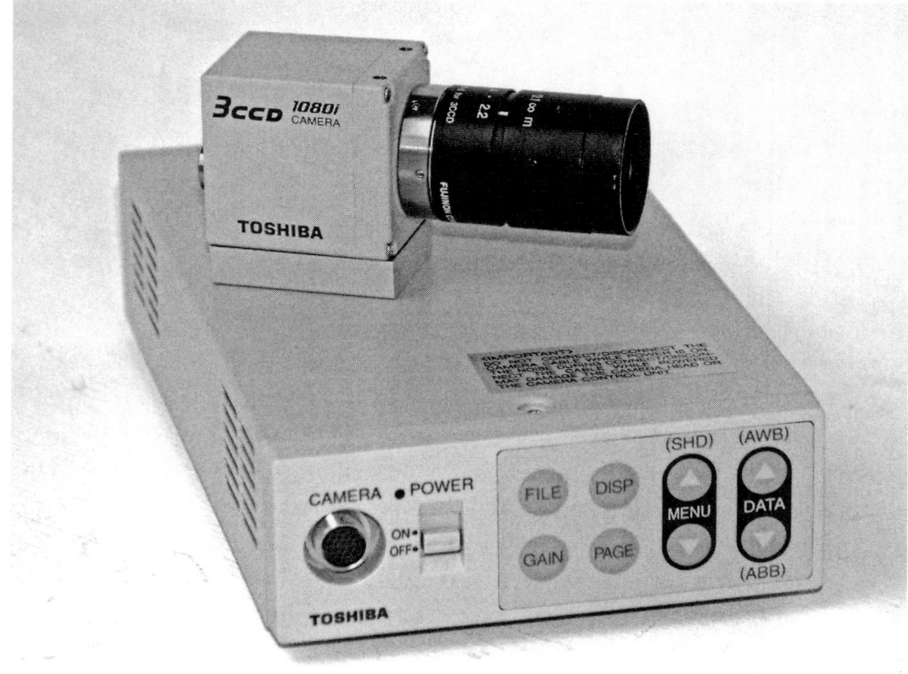

FIG 1.25
HD cam. "Toshiba's 3 CCD 1080i video camera."

OTHER LOCATION FILMING EQUIPMENT

Autocues and teleprompting machines can now be fitted to smaller cameras and used on location. New technology has allowed the once bulky units to sit on smaller prosumer kits and be carried around with ease (Figure 1.26).

FIG 1.26
Prompter on Canon camera. "I spotted this neat unit at the Video Forum exhibition. It's mounted on a lightweight tripod head and mates up to a Canon XL1 camera, perfect for taking into offices of CEOs and other corporate work. It will also give your amateur presenters an air of professionalism that working without a script denies them."

FIG 1.27
Z1 with top light fitted. "SONY HVR-Z1e with top light fitted. Great on a tripod but is too heavy for handheld work. The ergonomics of a camera are as important as the pictures it produces. A badly balanced video camera will spend more time in a locker cupboard than out on a shoot."

CHAPTER 2

Setting Up Location Monitors and Cameras

Many people get shown how to set up camera viewfinders and monitors when they do their basic camera training, but if you have missed this or simply didn't have time for it then this chapter will give you a good idea of how to do it and why it's important. At times when you are shooting away, say, in other countries, you might be using hired-in cameras and monitors or working in difficult conditions, or the kit you are traveling with might have been dropped or knocked and will need resetting. And if you don't understand how to correctly adjust the viewfinder or monitor manually when you are out in the field, then you stand a real chance of recording overexposed or underexposed pictures.

When you come to shoot a scene or start lighting a new setup, it's important that your camera viewfinder and any monitors are showing a similar image and that they all match each other in terms of brightness, contrast, and color saturation. It can happen that in a busy crew room someone can just grab a camera at the last minute and go out to shoot straightaway with it. Now without checking the viewfinder to see if it is set up properly you could end up overcorrecting the scenes and the shots will be badly exposed. So unless you know the basics of setting up the viewfinders and screens then you are taking a gamble that might not pay off.

To emphasize how important this is, let's take the example of trying to get a correct exposure through your video camera of a scene when the brightness in the viewfinder has been set way too low, and also we'll assume that the zebra patterning does not work on this hypothetical camera. What will happen is that you'll look through the viewfinder and see the image, which will be quite dark and contrasty. So you will quite rightly open up the iris to get a lighter image of the subject you are shooting that will then seem better exposed. What you have done in effect is to overcompensate for the viewfinder's overly dark picture, unfortunately overexposing the image, which is then being recorded on tape or disk. It would be the same mistake if the viewfinder brightness were wound up too high; you would then stop the camera down to make the image darker and you would then be underexposing the final shot. The same applies if you are using a monitor to check your shots and it is also incorrectly set up. So it pays to do some checks before shooting.

If a DP (director of photography in the U.S., DOP in the U.K.) is lighting a large set with many lights, he will want to view monitors that all register the same in terms of brightness, contrast, and color. The problem he will have if the monitors are not set up correctly is either overlighting or underlighting the scene, and this will lead to inconsistent lighting levels on the set.

At the moment in video we all work with a mixture of monitors. Many ENG cameras use black and white viewfinders, others have LCD screens, some studio floors use CRT tubed monitors, and other tech areas have black and white monitors as well, not to mention computer screens that can accept a video signal and again are used for monitoring purposes.

So first things first, let's look at the tried and tested way of setting up a camera's small black and white monocular viewfinder ready for shooting in any conditions.

First turn the camera to bars.

Among the three main switches, brightness, contrast and peaking, first turn the peaking down so there is not too much detail in the bars and the image does not appear too artificial. For more information on the peaking control, see chapter 3, table 3.2.

Then wind down both the brightness and the contrast so the bars become increasingly darker in the viewfinder. Do this in stages by taking the brightness down slightly and then the contrast; keep doing each one in turn until the screen is dark or has lost most of its image.

Now wind in a small amount of contrast and then stop at a point where you can just make out the first two or three bars and the left side of the frame or the raster. Now bring up the brightness slightly so you can see more bars to the

FIG 2.1
Viewfinder controls. "Standard viewfinder controls on a SONY ENG camera. These are on a DigiBetacam viewfinder, but do you know how to adjust them correctly out in the field?"

right. What you are aiming for is to see all bars from left to right without the first, white bar being overbright and the final bar, black, being too dark and looking as if it mates with the bar to its left. A correctly set up viewfinder has all eight bars (PAL, phase alternating line) visible and is not too "milky," i.e., the contrast is too low. All bars stand out equally and do not seem to fade into the ones next to them. The reason for adjusting the brightness and contrast in small amounts alternatively is to detect when the final image looks correct and to know that an equal amount of brightness and contrast has been wound into this image, not too much of one or the other. Finally adjust the peaking to the level that allows you to see some detail coming through. With camera bars switchd on the peaking should be visible and affect the edges between each bar. With bars switched off the peaking will affect the edges of all your subjects in the frame and when peaking is turned to the lowest position will give a soft edge between the items in the frame and turned to the highest position will show more detail to these edges. It's your personal preference where you have this adjusted to and it's purpose is to help you find focus comfortable on all different types of shots and subjects.

The same technique can be applied to location monitors as well. When I was researching this topic I asked some manufacturers of modern LCD screens, large and small, how they would adjust their screens to show a true image.

Most thought the old way I have described above would be effective; however, some screens now have self-calibration modes and do it for you but these will give you the default factory setup, which should be fine, but you can then apply the manual method above to make some fine adjustments. LCD screen makers did offer some interesting points about their screens such as the fact that TFT screens are backlit and have a limited gamma range in the yellow range and a higher one in the red range. LCDs measure their brightness in candelas (NITS in the U.S.) and a 500-candela screen would be effective for location work although 700–1000 candela screens are becoming available.

A well-set up camera viewfinder, even though it's black and white, should give you a correct range of tones to work with from light to dark, and when it does, you will automatically set the iris at the correct level (Figures 2.2–2.4).

Till now we've been concentrating on setting up equipment in the field but it's well worth having a video engineer correct your settings before any important trip happens. This will give you an accurate match between your camera viewfinder and any monitors you use. For U.S. cameramen who need to set up their NTSC (National Television System Committee) equipment take a look at the description given by Barry Braverman in his Focal Press book *Video Shooter*. He goes into a lot of good tech information about the U.S. kit.

Most video cameras – small or large, pro or domestic – will allow you access to deeper adjustments such as Gamma, detail, black stretch and black level, etc.

FIG 2.2
Bars set correctly… "Well-set up viewfinder with bars giving an even reading of brightness, saturation, and contrast from left to right, white to black."

FIG 2.3
Bars at the start of adjustment. "With the brightness and contrast wound right down to a very small level you can then start to adjust them both upward, contrast first, in small increments."

FIG 2.4
Bars about 50% adjusted. "About half way to the correct working level."

If you have a good understanding of video engineering, then you'll know the reasons for altering these and what it will do to your final recorded pictures. But I've come across many enthusiastic amateur video engineers in my years of filming who are happy to tweak away on location, changing all the adjustments until they find that magical look they are after only to find that when the shots are viewed in the edit suite they aren't as brilliant as was thought while shooting.

There is also a real danger that if the settings are not put back to normal at the end of the day, then the next cameraman to use the kit ends up with results he really doesn't want. My advice is to have the camera setup correctly once a year and only change it when needed and by a good engineer using scope and grade one monitors.

PLUGE

This intriguing acronym stands for "picture line up generation equipment"... It's an another useful tool to help set the brightness of video monitors. They come in a range of different formats but are usually a set of bars – super black, normal black, mid-gray, and white – all close together. You'll find them incorporated in some cameras, bars generators such as the SONY HVR-Z1e (Figure 2.5) or the SONY DSR 450. If the screen is set too low, then it will appear that the two black bars look the same with no visible difference between them. If the screen is set too high, the three bars appear black.

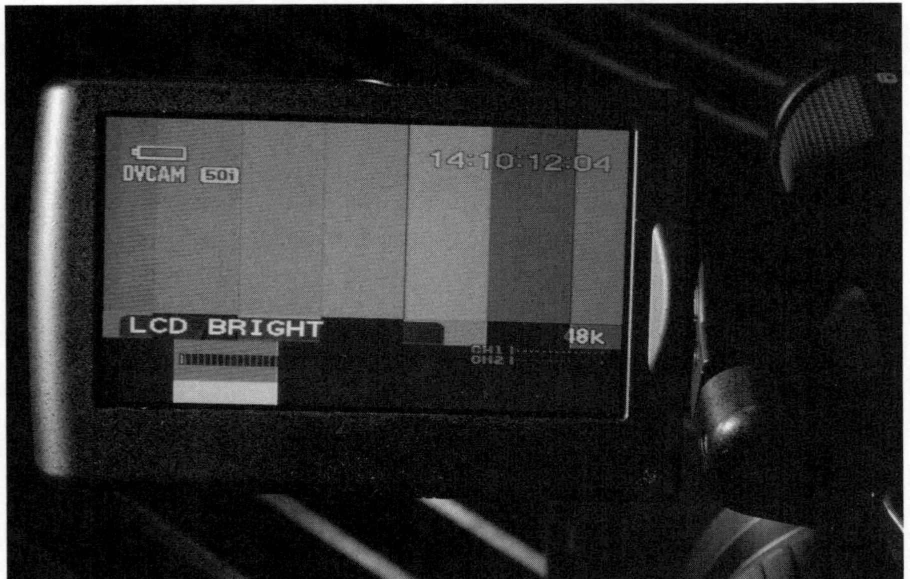

FIG 2.5

NTSC bars on SONY HVR-Z1e. "This set of bars comes from a SONY HVR-Z1e. This particular camera is a U.K. model but the format of bars it produces is the U.S. standard as seen on NTSC. It does not mean the camera is an NTSC camera. The Z1 only has one control for its pull-out screen and that is for brightness. Check to make sure that this is set around 50% as it is in this shot and giving a correct setup to shoot with."

So that's all well and good for adjusting cameras and monitors that have separate brightness, contrast, and peaking adjustments, but many new cameras now have LCD screens with only one adjustment, usually the brightness (Figure 2.6). Some of the flip-out screens housed in the camera can give a false impression; color can seem oversaturated on a small screen and all items in the frame seem to be in focus on wide shots and brightness can be misleading.

So how can we best set these up? A good rule of thumb is to have the brightness at 50% as a starting point. Then adjust it up or down to compensate for the light and the conditions that you are working in. Obviously a darkened room will need a less bright viewfinder and a sunny day will need more brightness. But as before adjust it in small increments until you reach a good workable level and never shoot with the viewfinder brightness turned right up or right down.

The SONY 450 DSR DVCAM also has a flip-out LCD screen plus the normal black and white viewfinder. The LCD only has preset positions – off, low, and high – but the optical viewfinder has the normal set of adjustments.

Zebra patterning is there to help you see when the shot is overexposed, but many cameramen do not like working with this on. This is a personal decision

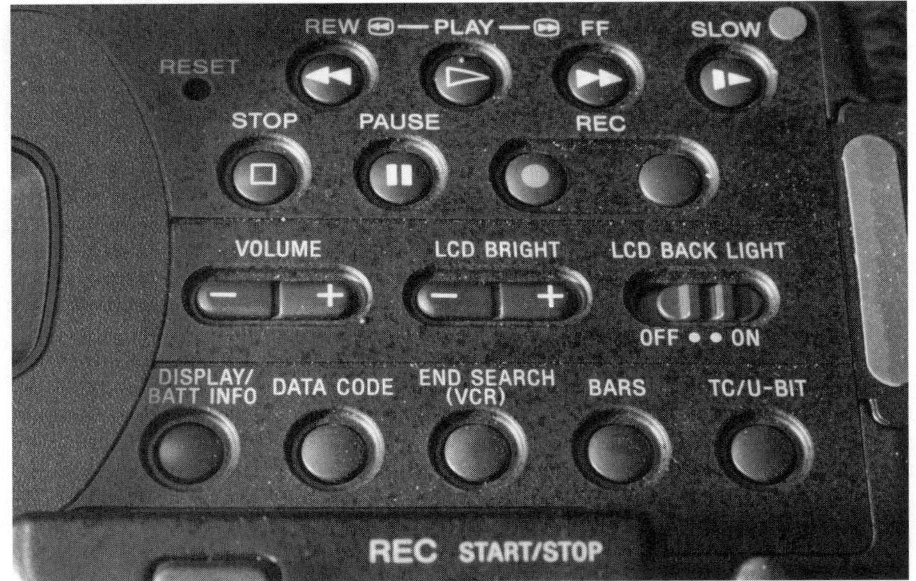

FIG 2.6
Brightness control on Z1. "This adjustment on the SONY HVR-Z1e is to be found on the right side of the flip-out LCD screen; it only affects the brightness of the pull-out LCD screen and not the monocular viewfinder."

but the zebra is, in effect, a very useful tool to help find the correct aperture. It's not just something that you use when you are starting out as a cameraperson and then stop using when you get more experienced. Even pro cameramen with many years of experience will use the zebra if they have to shoot with a camera that is new to them.

However some locations can have very difficult lighting conditions to cope with, and if you are used to how the zebra works in normal conditions then it can be used as a confidence check on these tricky scenes. Think of it more as a tool to keep your exposure as precise as possible and help in strange lighting conditions. For example let's assume that your subject is correctly lit but the background is very bright or too dark. The zebra will give you the confidence to keep the subject correctly exposed while the background goes over or under in exposure. And if this background becomes far too bright to work with the zebra will let you know this and you can decide how best to solve this problem.

TIP
Most video editors say that they can adjust video pictures that are underexposed to a better degree than pictures that are overexposed. This is because the overexposed shots normally lose some detail in the highlight areas and this detail can't be pulled back in as it's gone forever, whereas the underexposed shots still retain some information and this can then be raised in the edit suite. So if you are going to make a mistake then choose the right mistake...underexpose every time. That's what the film cameramen had to do when shooting a reversal film; they exposed for the highlights in the scene, those that were the brightest, not the average area of brightness or the middle areas.

Editors also tell me that, thanks to clever nonlinear editing systems, nowadays they can also correct shots that have the wrong color balance on them, but only to a limited degree. If you've just come from shooting a nice, warm, cozy fireside scene indoors with a color temp of 2800 K and then shot an outside interview in cloudy conditions (about 8000 K upward) without altering the color balance, then expect that lovely artistic blue look that you've just recorded to be permanent. You could always tell the producer that it was an effect filter…

However the only way to be sure is to white balance in the light source you are shooting under. It's important to get it as correct as possible on location because leaving it to the video editor to correct in postproduction is really not a good working practice.

Most location cameras allow the zebra to be set at different levels, the common settings being 75%, 90%, and 95%. So it's important to check what setting your camera is set to before shooting or once again you could over- or under-expose your shots.

If you are not quite sure how and why the zebra works then the following information will help you.

Let's start by assuming that we have framed an MCU (medium close-up) of a person in our viewfinder.

A viewfinder with a zebra that is set to 75% will show its stripes on the side of the face where the key light (or sun) is coming from. And when the camera is correctly exposed the stripes will cover a fair area of that side of the face and also other parts of the frame, which have the same or even more brightness. At 90% the stripes will appear but will cover much less of the face and only other areas of the screen that are at 90% of the total brightness. At 95% you will only see the stripes just coming through, perhaps on the white collar of a person's shirt and brighter areas of the background. There is no right or wrong position out of these three settings; it's down to you to decide which one works best for the shooting you do.

My personal preference is for a zebra of 95% as it only shows on a small proportion of the screen and doesn't distract me from other areas of work. Shooting locations can vary so much with different types of light that the zebra acts as a constant reference or benchmark, so I know where to set my exposure and I'm not fooled by working in challenging lighting. Once you get used to it you'll find that you quickly start to set the iris manually to exactly the right level for any given shot, and this is again something that you can take with you to any type of video camera – large or small.

Sometimes the zebra level of the camera you are using can be ascertained from simply switching onto bars. If it's set at 75% then you'll see the second bar from the left, yellow, seen in the Figure 2.7 as gray, has the stripes showing on it.

FIG 2.7
Bars with stripes on the gray one. "Seventy five percent bars as seen in the viewfinder."

Every cameraman I have ever known has a forthright

opinion one way or another about which level of zebra works best, but at the end of the day just use the level that suits you best and gives you the most confidence in your exposure and lighting.

CAMERA GAIN

Talking of cameramen having forthright opinions, here's another one that gets people frothing at the mouth: using gain. Virtually all cameras, whether pro or consumer, allow you to switch gain into the picture. The idea being that if you are running out of light to shoot with then this gain will give you another stop or so of light to work with. But like everything else we have spoken about in this book, it's not what you use but how you use it that matters. On today's cameras with advanced circuitry, a small amount of gain will not be visible to the end user. So if you put 3 dB of gain in because, for example, you need to shoot a subject on the tight end of the lens and it's getting darker outside, then it's unlikely that anyone viewing the tape will notice this small amount of lift to the pictures, unless it's a retired video Engineer with a vectorscope linked to his TV. A lot of cameras allow you to select which set of gain levels are applied to the gain switch so, for instance, you could have 0, 3, 6 dB or 3, 6, 9 dB. It all depends on what you shoot.

A clever use of gain is when the camera allows you to dial in −3 dB, which will help limit the picture noise inherent in the dark areas of the frame. So if you've just picked up that spare camera from your colleague, last minute, it will pay to check what his settings are.

TIP

We have to shoot a lot of live interviews in the evening or at nighttime at Westminster using the Parliament building as a background, and it is very poorly lit at nighttime. These shots go into the main news bulletins and current affairs shows. Instead of overlighting the foreground subjects, which would lead to the background building becoming even blacker in the frame, we use a small light, say, a 150 W, with a diffusion filter over it, and work with the camera nearly wide open, about f2.0. Then we switch in 3 dB of gain to show some extra detail in the background Parliament building. This leaves the presenter correctly exposed, the background looks great because it is not overlit but you can see enough detail in it, and this background is then slightly soft in focus compared to the presenter so he or she stands out in the final frame. Millions of people every night see these shots and no one has complained yet.

When you look at a new scene before shooting, half close your eyes and search for the different tones of brightness from dark to very bright and look for a mid-or average area within the scene. Nine out of ten times this will end up as the midpoint for your exposure. This is one of the points expounded upon by that wonderful photographer Ansel Adams who developed a whole technique for judging tones within scenes called the "zone system." When you look closely at his pictures you'll see lots of details in both highlights and dark areas.

Inspiration for video shooting indeed.

SETTING UP TIME-CODE

Finally it's worthwhile talking about time-code for a while as it's one of the areas that video cameras and the whole production sequence rely upon. If you are new to video workflow or want to know how it's approached in the broadcast TV industry then read on. If you know your way around this topic then please skip ahead.

Time-code is the reference point on the tape or hard disk that follows right through the whole production process. Lots of people rely on it and if it goes wrong, becomes nonsequential, or jumps then it affects viewing, off-line editing, graphics, sound dubs, and on-line editing and causes an awful lot of bad language from video editors, which I've found to my cost…

Think of it like this: when you've shot your lovely footage of a Ferrari coming around a couple of hairpin bends, say you've done five separate takes of the same thing, and you decide to use the start of take one along with the end of take three. The best way to let everybody else in the team know exactly what shots you want used in the edit is to give them time-code numbers, which are individual to every frame you have recorded; then you don't have to explain it in words many times over.

Basically the four fields of time-code in your LCD screen or viewfinder reflect hours, minutes, seconds, and fields so every shot has its unique reference point and time-code number. They look like something this: 02:10:19:11.

You can set your camera to run time-code in two ways: record run, which is when you press the record button on the camera, it will start and it will then stop when you turn the record button to off; or secondly to free run, when the code runs constantly whether the camera is recording or not. And there are few good reasons why you can choose one setting over the other.

Standard Location Single Camera Shooting

When you start shooting a project and you know you will record more than one tape and you will be moving from location to location, the industry standard would be to start with time-code on tape one at 01:00:00:00. You would use the "record run" setting on the time-code and the code would only be laid down as you hit the record button and stop when you stopped recording. Every time you change tapes, you dial in the next tape number on the first two digits, i.e., 02:00:00:00 then the next tape starts with the digits 03: the next tape with 04: etc., so everyone involved in the production process now knows that the tape box, or hard disk box, labeled 01 matches up with the tape that has time-code starting with 01. When you view the many tapes you've shot and write down your rough edit list then you know it's the first one. When the off-line editor wants to start the first cut he knows it's tape one, day one. When the on-line editor comes to assemble the show he knows it's tape one, day one. When the graphics guy wants to find the rushes so he can quickly pull off the right frame, he knows it's tape one…Everyone knows where to find the exact shot on tape one recorded on day one and it saves loads of time, even when the tape is put back in the wrong box…Another point worth remembering is that it's always good practice to record 10–30 seconds of bars at the head of each new tape or disk, and if you can also put tone on the audio tracks at the same time then the video editor can line up his edit machines to your bars and adjust the audio levels to read the same.

So Why Bother with Continuous Time-Code?

The following are the two reasons.

RUNNING TWO CAMERAS TOGETHER IS AN EFFECTIVE WAY TO RECORD IMPORTANT INTERVIEWS

The benefits are that there is no need to record any reverses or, the presenter's questions or reactions after the main interview has happened, and you get a more accurate recording of the event. Now you can do this using record run time-code as we looked at above, but if you use this method there will be different time-codes recorded on both cameras as it's almost impossible to keep them running together with synchronous time-code. So using free run time-code you can record exactly the same time-code onto both cameras/tapes/disks. This means that the video editor can edit in and out of both tapes at exactly the same point using the time-code from either camera and without having to search visually for a matching edit point, which makes the edit so much smoother and faster.

To set this up you:

- Decide which camera will be the master camera
- Switch this camera's time-code to the free run position
- Plug in a BNC cable to the time-code output socket of this camera
- Plug the other end into the time-code input socket of the second, slave, camera
- Then switch the slave camera to free run as well
- Check that the slave camera is now reading exactly the same time-code as the master camera
- When this is confirmed unplug the BNC lead from both cameras
- If either camera has to change batteries resync the code using the same process as above as this can cause the time-code settings to drift apart

RECORDING AN EVENT THAT RELIES ON TIME OF DAY

A big conference or music concert where certain acts or events happen over a planned period of time might be better recorded with time of day, free run code, as standard, especially if more than one camera is being used. Again the editor can use the synchronous time-code on each and any camera tape and simply mark an edit point using this code rather than searching for a visual matchup of the action on different cameras.

The only drawback to time of day code used to be that it took longer for the cameras to lock up after pressing the record button, but that's not a problem on long events.

ANY OTHER PROBLEMS WITH TIME-CODE

If you have a gap in your time-code, you might have played back a good take to show the producer in the camera and not cued it up at the last frame when the viewing has ended; then some edit suites will have problem handling the gap in time-code which will stop the machine performing a clean edit. They use the time-code to control their tape position and gaps can confuse them. Also on nonlinear suites the machines can simply stop playing in the rushes if they come across a time-code gap and you'll end up with nothing there, just black space. So for such a simple little thing you can now see that there are pitfalls to be aware of.

DROP FRAME TIME-CODE

Just to complicate matters you need to be aware that time-codes used in America for NTSC recording come in two distinct flavors: drop frame and nondrop frame.

The U.K. system, which is PAL time-code, is at 25 fps but the U.S. NTSC time-code is at 29.97 fps, which means you need to know about drop frame and nondrop frame time-code modes.

This rate of 29.97 fps is slightly slower than the 30 fps, which would then tie in happily with the U.S. frequency rate. This rate was decided upon when the changeover from black and white to color video was happening and the added color information would sometimes clash with other parts of the signal such as the audio. So the existing audio rate was left the same but the video parts were altered. As the rate of 29.97 fps is less than the 30 fps, a small time discrepancy over any length of video will happen, so a method of compensating for this was worked out; drop frame is the way chosen to deal with it.

Time-code recorded in drop frame mode only drops the code numbers that match the frames of video captured, not the actual frames of video themselves. It is an industry recognized SMPTE (Society of Motion Picture and Television Engineers) code that runs accurately over normal clock time and loses, or *drops*, two frames of code (every 60 seconds apart from every 10 minutes where it jumps then). This compensation allows it to keep to normal clock time. You can recognize drop frame code being played on video machinery as the viewable digits are separated by semicolons in the display screen like this: 01;00;00;00, whereas nondrop frame code uses colons in between the numbers like this: 03:00:00:00.

NONDROP FRAME RECORDING

Nondrop frame recording, which is again an SMPTE code, doesn't use this compensation, and relates with 30 fps. This method means that it does not match clock time exactly and the length of a video section is always shorter. For every 10 minutes, there will be an 18 frame difference.

TV stations taking in NTSC recorded programs for transmission will normally require the master tapes to have drop frame time-code.

CHAPTER 3

Operating Tips and Techniques

The debate on choosing the best camera will go on forever and choosing the best kit to operate on a daily basis will never be straightforward. Most of your decisions will be based on the type of work you shoot, your budget, which editing system you use, and your clients' requirements for which recording format they use. As mentioned in Chapter 1 the amount of video cameras on the market today to choose from is huge (see chapter 1), and after making this choice we are still left to work out which recording format will be the best. If you work for more than one client or TV station, the chances are that you'll be expected to work with many different kits and cameras, and if a really nice job comes in, let's say you've been asked to shoot a glossy corporate production with high-end production values on location, you will be expected to work with a high-end camera kit, which you might not be used to.

So we're left with a bit of a problem as operators. We need to be able to work effectively with as many of today's kits as possible and be confident while doing it. Depending on what you shoot and for whom you shoot, this range of cameras could go from palmcorders to PD170s SONY HVR-Z1es, Canon XL-1Hs, through to DSR 570/450's DigiBeta, and HDCAMs, and possibly you'll want to shoot on film if a job comes up. Again if you are or intend to become a freelancer you'll make more money if you can do more jobs and turning down a shoot because you are not sure of how to work the client's video kit is not going to be helpful for you.

To start solving this dilemma we will need to get a standard system of working that we can apply to any kit, from the smallest consumer camera to high-end pro units. If we can develop a consistent way of shooting that works effectively on a day-by-day basis, no matter what the kit is, then we can use this standard way of working on any camera. But you must keep it simple and straightforward; the more complicated you make your working practice, the more likely you are to make mistakes or slow down during a busy shooting day. The whole idea of this process is to keep the camera operator in control of the shoot and not worry unduly about the kit he is using.

The talent is in the cameraman/woman not the camera. No matter how clever and sophisticated the camera is it is still only a box that gathers the images that the operator tells it to. The camera kit is the hardware but it can't function unless it's got access to the software…that's you, you're the clever bit….

After this it is simply a question of gaining the relevant extra knowledge needed to shoot with more complicated video kits or use advanced functions when they are needed. And this is why it is crucial to understand the primary shooting functions used on every shoot and be able to ignore the many extras and gizmos that camera manufacturers are tempting us with until the time comes to use them. If we apply this process of keeping it simple and ignoring the functions that are either over complicated, irrelevant, and buried deeply in menus or time consuming to access then it is possible to get good results from a wide range of cameras and even use the most complicated, high-end camera effectively.

A normal day's location shooting will be driven by time, or the lack of it. Again and again we will be expected to shoot many setups, scenes, or locations in a day; each shoot must be done well and be of a consistent and reasonable standard but the time to get each setup lit correctly, audio worked out, moves checked, etc., seems to get less and less. So it makes sense to develop a way of working that is simple and straightforward and that you can trust to give you good results. This way you can be confident that your rushes will be good and the footage usable.

And my point here is that this will not happen on nine out of ten shoots if the cameraman is slowed down by having to access different menu options for audio, gain, shutter, aperture, etc., or if he's continually trying out new camera functions. You can lose plenty of time and you can put yourself in a position where mistakes will be made. The answer is to know exactly which functions you need to use, know how to find them on each camera, and how to adjust them quickly and confidently. If you are not sure about them, then leave the experimenting for another day.

Once you've developed this system and know it works for you you, can start trying out advanced techniques using newer camera functions and learning about high-end shooting subtleties. You will be safe in the knowledge that however difficult and arduous the shoot becomes you can always fall back on your newly developed standard way of working and produce good results whatever happens, and if you are on a really rushed schedule and have a hard day then you'll be glad that this simple, straightforward method of filming allows you to get results time and time again.

Table 3.1 gives you an "at a glance" check of every setting up item that needs to be done before, during, and after shooting a take on a video camera. If you are new to shooting, then use it as a checklist and method of working. Try to do things in exactly the same order when you set up your shots and scenes before recording and soon you will find yourself with a foolproof method of shooting. You can then make your own list from mine using the ones that apply to your shoots and will quickly find that your filming will become more consistent with less room for errors. This will lead to better shots and give you more time to concentrate on lighting, nice moves on the camera, and other creative options.

Table 3.1 Method of Working Chart

A. Setting up

- Decide where your subjects are going to be placed in the location, bear in mind:
  Backgrounds – are they complementary. Look out for any tall items that might "grow" out of people heads. Is the background overbright and will it cause problems with exposure?

  Presenters in front of sunsets can be a particular problem…
- Camera position
  Can you get the camera 2–3 m away from your subject or will you be forced closer because of walls, posts, etc., in the way? If you are forced nearer will this mean that you are shooting on the very wide end of your zoom lens? If so make sure that your subjects' faces don't look distorted and with that "fish eye" effect that you can start to get on a wide-angle lens.

  Position the guests and, if needed, mark this spot with a coin or similar so they know where to come back to if they have to leave shot.
- Ambient noise
  How noisy is the location? If it's too loud, say a busy road or near a construction site, will you be able to hear the subject's audio over this noise? If in doubt move away from the noise but keep the background you need still in shot, just farther away.
- Lighting
  With the background you want in shot does the sunlight fall on your subjects' faces satisfactorily or is it coming from behind them or at an odd angle? Will they need lighting, and if so, is power available for the lamps? Can you use a reflector instead?

(*Continued*)

Table 3.1 *(Continued)*

- Get the kit ready
  Place the tripod in the spot you need at the height you want to shoot and level up the tripod head.
  Put the camera into the base plate and switch it on.
  Check that you have enough battery power for the takes needed.
  Check that you don't have the lens extender (doubler) switched in.
  Dial in the filter you need then white balance and black balance.
  Check that the gain and shutter speeds are in the position you want them to be.
  Set time-code and lay bars if not done already.
- Choose mics and get XLR cables ready
  Mic up guests; make sure any leads are hidden from shot and the mics are clipped on neatly with cables hidden from view, and switch the camera to the correct audio input.
  If you are plugging external mics into the rear of the camera, when you do your sound level just double-check that you are not listening to the camera top mic. If you are in a quiet location this top mic should give very good sound (but not as good as your external mics) and you could be fooled into thinking that you are monitoring the external mics… (*Most pro cameramen have made this mistake, including me…and no matter what any cameraman tells you he/we have all left the tape stock at home and forgotten to white balance at least once in our careers…probably many more.*)
  Get a sound level from each mic and check levels into the camera are correct and on manual.
- Double-check the shot and only say you are ready to record when you have double-checked, never before. Don't be rushed into turning over until you are quite ready. You now control the shoot and what happens when.

B. Run to record

- Double-check that the tally/record light is on and time-code is running.
- Make sure the guests haven't moved position.
- Check audio levels now and again on your meters throughout the take; they should be around −18 dB.
- When the take is finished keep recording for an extra five or so seconds, then stop.

C. Playing back/confirming the take

- Can be a good idea to do this on the first take of the day to confirm that both video and audio have been laid down correctly and there is no sign of breakup on the video and audio tracks, but if you have a busy day ahead it becomes tiresome to keep doing it. The big thing to remember here is that after you have played back the shot and everyone has seen it always park the tape at the end of the last shot. And if you've stopped the playback at a point that is not the end of the tape, say it was 1/4 way in, you will need to shuttle the take up to the end position or you will over-record the existing take with the next one you record and also have noncontinuous time-code… (*and we've all done this more than once as well…*).
- Get to the end point of the last take then press the "return" button on your lens, which will run the tape back to the last frame and re-queue it to the correct point.

D. Using more than one tape

- Sometimes clients will ask you to stop using the existing tape and put a new one in for the next record, which is possibly as they want to take this tape away for editing straight after the shot is done or use it for certain shots later on in the shoot. No problem here unless you are

Table 3.1 *(Continued)*

asked to put the first tape back into the camera after the second tape has been whisked away by your client. The camera time-code will now be registering a different set of numbers to the time-code laid down on the last shot of your first tape…so if you shoot straightaway you'll have noncontinuous time-code laid down on this tape.

- The solution is to make a note of the last time-code of the first tape and write it on the tape box when you are swapping tapes. Then you simply reset the camera time-code to the same number that you made a note of when you replaced the first tape. This will ensure that no jumps appear on your recorded time-codes.

Table 3.2 lists the primary functions that we are interested in for day-by-day working on video cameras. If you have not come from a camera-based background or need some more information on what they do and why they do it, then refer to this chart to help your knowledge.

Table 3.2 Primary Functions and Working Techniques

Function	Details/techniques
White Balance:	
Whatever camera you are shooting with, always standardize the way you do the white balance. Always use the manual setting where possible and balance to the light source that you are shooting with, or the one that directly lights your subject. Standardize your routine for white balancing. Don't use a preset on one camera, a custom setting on another, and manual on another. It's too complicated, you'll end up forgetting which is which, and it can lead to mistakes.	Most cameramen will agree that on ENG cameras it is always best to use the white/black buttons and not the preset positions, and always rewhite balance when you shoot a scene in a different location or different light source. This cover 98% of all shooting situations but there will be some locations where it's not practical to do this and you will have to use presets. An example would be shooting under stage or theater lights where you can't get a white light to balance to. Many of these lights will probably have colored gels on them to give color effects to different parts of the stage that will make life difficult for anyone trying to do a manual white balance under a standard "white" light. Check with the light technicians to see if they are using tungsten lights (3200 K) or daylight (5600 K) and then set your camera preset to the position needed; if you have a color monitor then use this to double-check that it looks correct. Another example would be shooting sunsets and sunrises. If you manually color balance while the sun/set/rise is happening you will lose the lovely warm tones so here again, try a preset position of 5600°K, which will let the rich colors stand out.
	On the smaller prosumer cameras again try and use the same routine. Always balance to a white sheet lit by the scene's major light source. Again don't use the preset positions unless there is a good reason for doing so. If you are shooting multiple cameras in these examples check to make sure that you are all using the same preset position.

(Continued)

Table 3.2 *(Continued)*

Function	Details/techniques
	A lot of people I have talked to think that by leaving the white balance on auto it will give a correct color every time, but this is not the case, especially if your scenes are lit by multiple, different light sources.
	There are very good reasons for adopting this routine: First, it will standardize the way you set up the camera before each scene and you won't have to search for extra presets that might be hidden in menus. Secondly, when you work in an environment that is not controllable, such as an office, factory, or other similar workspace, a lot of the available light is from mixed sources; you might have daylight from a nearby window added to a ceiling light and then you may be adding your own light to shoot your subject. Using a manual balance each time will allow you to get the color on the subject correct. If you don't you'll simply get a shot that is broadly color balanced but your subject could be too warm or too cold depending on which light is falling on him or her.
	Everyone manages to forget to balance at some time or another, especially on busy days, but if you use these techniques and rebalance frequently then when you do forget to do a white on one scene the chances are that you will remember for the next scene, so only one scene will have the wrong color on it.
	Also it will then become an automatic thing for you to do after changing locations and that means that even on the busiest, most frantic days you will not make mistakes and, for example, shoot a daylight scene using the color balance you last did, which might have been a tungsten room, and if you did you'll see a lovely blue tinge to all the daylight footage. Very artistic.
	By using this method you will avoid the mistake of having set the color balance on, for example, a preset daylight position for the outside shots and left it there for all interior scenes during the rest of the day because you were distracted by other things. If you did you'll notice a lovely orange warmth creeping in over your footage.
	Lastly, another good reason for using this routine is for creative purposes. If you want to get more refined with your lighting and shooting you can subtly alter the warmth of the shot by white balancing through a 1/4 or 1/2 blue lighting control gel. This will result in a slightly warmer look to your shots.
	TIP If you carry a folded sheet of A4 white paper in your back pocket every day you shoot you'll be able to white balance quickly in any location without looking around for a white object or asking someone if they have one.

Table 3.2 *(Continued)*

Function	Details/techniques
Focusing	
Always use the manual focus setting.	This applies to the prosumer cameras as most ENG cameras are only manual focus.
	Sounds obvious but if you don't know how to switch the camera from auto to manual you'll waste a lot of time searching for the relevant switch, or it will be on auto and the first you know about it is when it starts adjusting itself during your shot.
	A good tip for getting a quick focus is to use the auto focus button that will get the camera in the right plane for correct focus, then switch to manual to do the final tweak. This way if you need to focus backward (or forward) slightly onto a different part of the frame you can set it up exactly.
Aperture	
Again, always use manual aperture but know how to switch it to and from auto.	The auto settings on modern cameras can be very good. I use mine when color balancing because it always sets the iris to the right position it wants for the balance, which saves me time. I'll also use it if I have to grab a shot very quickly in a new location. For example, we sometimes have to film the U.K. prime minister and his cabinet in the Cabinet Office for News clips, and for this job we are only given 3 minutes to complete the filming. After this a PR aide simply bundles us out of the room. So we roll tape before walking into the Cabinet Office, keep the iris on auto, and then every second out of the three minutes shooting schedule time can be used in the final edit.
	That said, if you leave it on auto for, lets say, an important exterior interview and the sun goes in (or comes out) on the background of your nicely framed shot then the camera will adjust for this change and the subject will be wrongly exposed. So check the shot on auto and then switch it to manual for the shooting. This way you can iris up or down if the light on your subject changes, but if the light on the background alters you can just leave the exposure alone and the subject stays correctly exposed. The main thing to remember here is that if you do need to alter the iris you must know which way to turn the aperture ring or adjuster. OK if it's on the lens but if it's on the body (HVR-Z1e) you'll need to know which way to go. Lastly, you need to be gentle with this adjustment; only adjust it fractionally at any one time so you don't go too far and the picture jumps in brightness or darkness. And watch out for cameras that have a "stepped" iris movement, not a linear ones, and if using one of these, only adjust it one step at a time. Use your zebra stripes to guide you to a correct exposure (see also Chapter 2).

(Continued)

Table 3.2 *(Continued)*

Function	Details/techniques
	I film many interviews outdoors in front of Big Ben and the Houses of Parliament and nine out of ten times our guests are in a hurry, have little time for the interview, and do not have any time to do retakes. No one is going to take kindly if I tell them that we need to reshoot because the sun went in or came out during the interview. It's imperative that I monitor the shot at all times and adjust the aperture up and down as needed. Try it a few times and you'll see how subtle you can be and your producers appreciate not having to retake the questions because of the change in light.
Gain	
Very useful tool at the right times and a hopeless one if it adjusts itself during your recording when you don't want it to.	ENG cameras switch gain in set increments. These steps can be −3dB, 0dB, 6dB, 9dB, and 12dB, and the switch is normally labeled low, medium, and high. On ENG cameras the gain button has to be physically switched on so it can't operate in auto mode and ramp up and down with lighting changes. Many cameras will allow you to alter the gain assigned to each position so don't just assume that low means 0dB and high means 9dB; it could be different so check in the camera's menu to see what the settings are. Some prosumer cameras have their gain functions on auto until they are switched off and some, such as the SONY HVR-Z1e, has the gain ganged to shutter and iris adjustments, and if you're not careful you can have these two on manual but the gain will still be on auto. You need to check that the gain is on manual on the Z1. When you are in manual, the display screen should show "gain," "iris," and "shutter." If any of these items are not highlighted the camera treats it as being in automatic mode and every time you alter the ones that are in manual this other one will adjust automatically to compensate.
	Normal shutter settings on a Z1 for the U.K. are 50 and for the U.S. 60. This is to match the field rates on the interlaced pictures and give a natural feel to the shots (see also Chapter 2).
	A modern camera can use 3dB and 6dB of gain without too much noise being evident on the final tape. It's useful if you want to help balance the lighting on the subject and the background and you can't alter the light falling on the background or if you want to keep the lighting at a low level allowing you to use a smaller wattage lamp, and have a soft background.
	TIP Sony DSR 500/570 and Ikegami DV7w and other cameras have a hyper gain button that jumps the gain up to a huge extent. I've never known anyone use this, except by mistake. If you pick up a camera and the viewfinder image is extremely noisy check this is switched off.

Table 3.2 *(Continued)*

Function	Details/techniques
Shutter	
Only use if there is a reason for it. If no reason then don't use it; it's one less adjustment to worry about. Some prosumer cameras have this switched on all the time so if you are using someone else's camera just check to see if the shutter is switched on and if it is what speed it is working at.	Most ENG cameras operate without the shutter on. If needed it can be turned on for a scene and then switched off at the end. Useful if you want to film a computer screen, which has a refresh rate different to your camera's normal shooting speed. You'll see the problem in the viewfinder; there will be roll bars apparent in the viewfinder or monitor when the camera is lined up on the screen. Using a variable shutter in the camera will normally get rid of these roll bars. But remember to open up the iris if the shutter speed gets higher as the camera will need more light.
	TIP Sometimes you'll find that the camera's shutter positions are not quite right and the roll bar is still visible on the screen. Try going into the screen's adjustments options and altering the screen rate from there.
	Again, if you share cameras in a busy crew room and you pick up someone else's camera check to see if the shutter is off.
	Some prosumer cameras have the shutter always on. If so pick a shutter speed that gives a normal look for normal shooting, say, 25 frames for U.K. filming and 30 frames for U.S. shooting.
	TIP You can create a nice effect by choosing a slower shutter rate. This gives a kind of "lag" to the movement in the camera. I used this a lot with a Canon XL1 when I was shooting mad motorcycling videos. We shot the bikes with the slow shutter speed and then slowed it down again in the AVID. The final result had a nice super 8 mm film feel to it and worked really well with music over the top.
Zebra	
Some people love the zebra, others hate it, but at the end of the day it's there to help you.	Most camera people are familiar with the zebra patterning, which can be switched on or off in the camera's viewfinder without being recorded onto tape. But a lot of new operators might not know how to get the best out of this seemingly simple iris aid.

(Continued)

Table 3.2 *(Continued)*

Function	Details/techniques
	The zebra exists to tell the operator how much light is falling on the subject. Too many zebra stripes indicate a lot of light and too few stripes indicate too little light. But you need to know at what point the zebra will start being visible, and you also need to find out how the zebra is set for the camera you are using.
	It used to be the case that Sony cameras always had their zebra's set for 75% and Ikegami's were set to 95%. This worked quite well because you always knew what to expect when using a different camera. Nowadays most cameras can allow the zebra to be adjusted for anything between 70% and 95% so, again, you need to check in the camera menu to see what that unit is set for. The percentage figure means that the zebra patterning will start to appear on the subject's face when the light falling on it gets to the set percentage.
	So for instance if you have your camera zebra set at 75%, then when the correct aperture is reached you will see these stripes. For example, if you have lit your subject with a key light from the right of the camera the zebra stripes will appear on the left of your subject's face (as the subject faces you) and the shadow side (the right side) will have less stripes or none depending on how hard and direct your lighting is. If you keep opening the iris past this point or adding more light the shot will become overexposed.
	A camera with its zebra set to 90% or 95% will have less zebra stripes visible on a correctly exposed subject than one set for 70% or 75% but the exposure will still be correct for that camera.
	The crucial point of this is that if you pick up a camera set to 90% zebra and you think it is set to 70% you'll overexpose all your shots if you allow the zebra to guide you.
	It's down to you what percentage zebra you work at, there's no right or wrong, but you may find that if you keep the zebra on all the time, then having it at 75%, and therefore apparent in the viewfinder most of the time, becomes a bit tiresome. If so try it at 90% and see how you get on.
	TIP A quick way of checking if the camera you've picked up has the zebra at 75% is by switching to bars. You should see the zebra appear on the second bar in from the left if it's on 75% (Figure 2.7).

Table 3.2 *(Continued)*

Function	Details/techniques
Peaking	Peaking is a control used mostly on ENG and larger cameras (Figure 1.15). As it is turned up or wound in from its lowest position you will see the edges of all the subjects and items in your viewfinder start to stand out more. The peaking is increasing the detail and artificially sharpening up the viewfinder (without altering or affecting the lens focus). It does this so the operator can get a better idea of what he is actually focussed on as the in-focus item will stand out against the other points slightly.
	When viewfinders have aged a bit they become softer to look at and therefore harder to use for critical focus. Using more peaking in an older viewfinder will help us to be confident about being correctly focussed. Many prosumer cameras do not have this facility. How much peaking to use is a personal decision as some people like it up high and others prefer it almost off. Think of it like the zebra, as a tool to help you work more confidently.

FOCUS PULLING LIKE THE PROS...

When I was a very junior cameraman at Trillion Video in London we shot many pop concerts and football matches. They were great to work on but were also fantastic for improving your powers of focussing on moving subjects. A lot of concerts back in the eighties were lit to give a dark eerie feeling and consequently there was not a lot of light falling on the band members. So if you were trying to hold close-ups of individual musicians as they moved around the stage it could be an uphill task to keep them in focus, especially when the cameras were working on a very wide aperture. Same again on gloomy Saturdays in the dead of winter when we were shooting football matches.

I used the experience of these outside broadcasts when I started shooting single camera location jobs, and the method I devised for keeping focus on a subject moving toward or away from my camera works time and again and will help to produce nice sharp shots on even the tightest of lenses and widest of apertures. It's best described in an example, and then you can refer to the photos below to work it out.

Let's say you are shooting a presenter walking toward you from about 20 m away. He's going to deliver his lines as he walks toward camera and the director wants to hold a mid-shot for the whole of the take, and he'll finish about four feet away from the lens, preferably nice and sharply focussed the whole way. We start by plotting the walk and timing the delivery of the lines, and we do this back to front.

1. Set up the end position that you want your presenter to reach when he will be nearest to your camera. Be careful that the background of the shot works well; try not to have any tall buildings "growing" out of the presenter's head or other types of distractions. Mark this position with a tape box or piece of camera tape so the presenter will be aware of the mark as he comes toward it (Figure 3.1).

FIG 3.1
The presenter at near point. "The presenter is at the end of his walk and nearest the camera."

2. Focus your lens for this position and put your finger on the focus ring on the lens and butt it up against the zoom servo box or a bar, both of which are static and won't move when you twist the focus. The idea being that you will use this static piece of the lens as a "stop" position and marker when the presenter hits his final mark, and you will be spot on focus. If you have a chinagraph pencil, then you can mark the focus ring at this position as well, or you could use camera tape (Figure 3.2).
3. Ask the presenter to deliver the lines while walking away from the camera and toward the area that you want the shot to start from. Get him to stop walking at the point that he finishe's the words. Don't be tempted to change focus on the camera yet; simply watch the walk and see where the presenter ends up and how fast he's walking. Some people prefer to walk quickly as it gives them a drive and pace that helps their delivery; others prefer a slower walk and more placid delivery. It's up to them (Figure 3.3).
4. Once he reaches an end spot get him to mark it with a coin or something similar so that it can't be seen in shot (if you are asked for a wider shot, that is).

FIG 3.2
A finger on the lens marking nearest point. "My finger has marked the focus point and is also touching the static zoom box. Now when Ian, my presenter, walks to this front position I will always be in perfect focus."

FIG 3.3
The presenter at far point. "Ian is now at the start position, farthest away from the camera, and ready to do a take. We know now that he will finish his words when he gets to the camera position marked earlier."

FIG 3.4
A finger on the lens focussed at the start point.
"Now refocus for the presenter's new position away from the camera. Again you can mark this point on the lens if you need to."

5. Now refocus on the presenter who is at his first mark and zoom in to hold a mid-shot…but don't take you finger off the focus ring while you do this. On most ENG lenses you'll be moving the focus ring down as you focus back onto the presenter in his position farthest away from you (Figure 3.4).
6. Rehearse the shot on tape. As your presenter moves toward the camera you focus forward (moving your left hand upward), the speed at which you move the focus ring toward your final, marked spot is governed by the presenter's walk so you might need to practice a couple of times. But assuming he walks at the same speed every time you'll soon know how fast you need to move your focus hand. And as long as he gets to his end mark or somewhere close to it, and you have your finger to rest against the end stop you are using, the shot will be in focus. To keep the shot size the same throughout the walk you will also have to zoom out while the presenter walks toward you. This is best done using a remote zoom attached to your pan handle as you can then zoom, pan, and tilt at the same time with your right hand. If you don't have a remote you need to zoom from the lens servo box with you right hand, and you'll need a bit of practice to do this smoothly.

You can look back at the taped rehearsal shot to see if you've done it right and also check if the shot is satisfactory, and then make any changes before you do a proper take. You can also show the director and presenter how it looks and

again make changes as needed. They will undoubtedly appreciate seeing the shot before it's recorded for real, and will also appreciate the trouble you've gone to set it out correctly. Another advantage is that they will know exactly how the shot will look when they come to edit. And this should rightly give you confidence in your work.

TIP

If you are using a smaller camera like a SONY HVR-Z1e then you need to remember that the focus ring does not have any end stops built into it, and it just keeps turning. Most people are used to lenses that have definite stop points: one at the nearest point of focus and the other at infinity, just like 35 mm stills cameras have. And we use these two stop points as a physical gauge of where we are in the whole focal range of the lens. To lose these two valuable marks is quite disconcerting (Figure 3.5).

Also bear in mind that on the Z1 the focus speed varies depending on how fast the ring is being turned. Fast turning results in quick changes from close to infinity, slow changes means that the focus only alters in very small distances.

And some lenses don't have a useful static point or raised area that you can use for an end stop and let your finger rest against. In this case you can always make a temporary one by using a small lump of blue-tack pushed into place.

FIG 3.5
Z1 focus adjuster. "SONY HVR-Z1e, which uses a focus ring that does not have any end stops, it just keeps on turning, and turning, and turning."

CHEATING THE EYELINE ON REVERSES WHEN YOU HAVE A BAD BACKGROUND

If you are filming people in a studio you will probably have a degree of control over where to position them, decide whether they should be sitting or standing, and what background they will be in front of. You can move them away from background items that will give a bad frame or simply distract the viewer, and create a pleasing frame, which can be lit correctly. However many locations, especially outside, will not allow you this degree of control and you will be limited to working with what's available.

If you are only filming one subject you have the option of moving him or her into a position where the background works well for the camera, but if you have to film reverse shots on the interviewer, the chances are that they will need repositioning to get the best frame. Especially if there is an unattractive highway or a broken down vehicle behind them.

The two key points to remember if you have to deal with this situation are that the shot sizes on the interviewer or "reverses" must match with the shots you have already filmed of the subject. So if you have filmed the first question on the interviewee as a mid-shot and all the following shots as MCU's (mid-close-ups), you'll need to use the same shot sizes on the interviewer questions.

See the section in Chapter 6, "Shot Sizes," for more information on this topic.

Secondly the camera should not cross the line or when you get to the edit both people will be looking the same way and not at each other. You've probably done this topic in your camera studies but it's easy to get caught out on location when you are doing interviews and moving positions frequently, especially, if you shoot the reverse shots after the interviewee has gone. In this case you can position the camera incorrectly and that's when you cross the line. I'll run through it here for those readers who need a quick refresher.

In Figure 3.6 we see our single camera A is shooting a normal two-handed interview. When he wants to turn around and shoot the reverse shots on the presenter he places the camera in position B.

TIP

If you have crossed the line, don't panic. Shoot some extra tight shots, perhaps hands and faces, so the editor can use them to cut in between shots.

Both people appear to be looking at each other when you view the two shots, which means it will edit

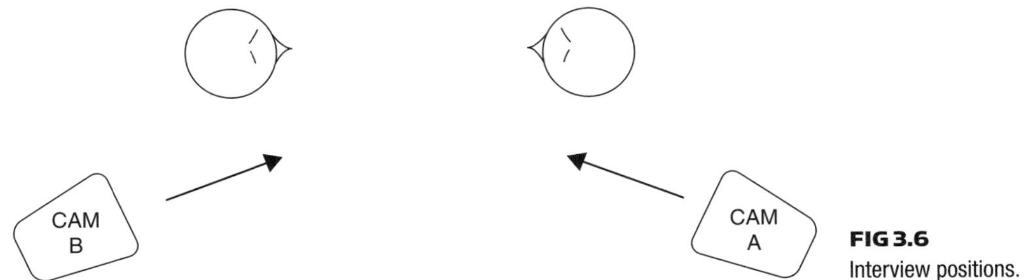

FIG 3.6
Interview positions.

correctly. However, if you were being rushed to shoot the reverses quickly, possibly you also had to cheat the background on the reverse shots, you might place the cameras as in Figure 3.7. Then when you viewed the shots back you would have both people looking in the same direction, and when edited together it would look like they were not looking at each other, so you've crossed the mythical line as seen in Figure 3.7.

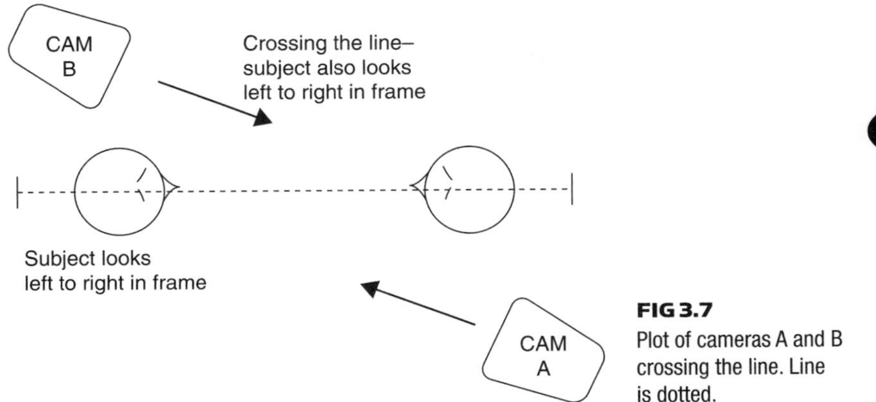

FIG 3.7
Plot of cameras A and B crossing the line. Line is dotted.

INTROS AND LONG PIECES TO CAMERA

Picture this. You are out filming with a presenter for the final sections needed to complete the evening's show, and the video editor needs all the rushes within the next hour to meet the TX deadline. The very last thing to shoot is the program's opening PTC (piece to camera) in which your presenter sets up the show, lists the items that the viewer will be watching, and links into the first clip. So it's important that it looks good and is word perfect.

The presenter wants a walking and talking shot, so she going to walk toward the camera, and you've just been shown the script…it's long…very long. She's just written it, there is no auto cue and now you've only got half an hour left to finish the shoot because…she's been writing it for the first half an hour. You work out the shot by timing the script as she reads it and then get her to pace it out, walking backward away from the camera so that she ends up at the right starting point for the walk. You rehearse it once and she gets about halfway through before forgetting the rest of the script. You try again and she falters at a different position, next time you record it and again it stops. What will you do to get this in the can?

Put in a turn to a magical, hypothetical camera 2…that's what we do. Split the script into two halves, preferably ending the first half at a point that makes sense for a cut. Tell the presenter to turn left (or right if that's what you want) and pretend she will be looking at this mythical camera 2. Make sure you end the first shot on a frame size that will cut to the new camera position; for this example we'll say a MS (mid-shot). After the presenter has turned to this new nonexistent camera you cut tape and move position to become camera 2. Get the presenter to do the last bit of the walk and overlap her last few words. Frame her in a MCU (Medium close up) and record the second half of the script. The sequence should end up looking good; the presenter can relax as she has now got two small script pieces to do and not one long one, and the video editor has a simple edit to do…. Everyone should be pleased…especially you.

ONE-MAN BAND…AUDIO…WHEN YOU ONLY HAVE ONE RADIO MIC

If you get caught shooting two people walking and talking and you only have one mic clip it on the inside lapel of one person but pointing directly in between the two people. You will find that as they talk to each other, they naturally turn their heads to each other, which will direct the audio to the mic (Figure 3.8).

DEALING WITH UNUSUAL PROBLEMS

Sodium Light Sources

Every different location throws up interesting challenges with lighting but most are solved by adapting your normal techniques to suit the situation. However, sometimes a shoot takes place in problematic locations and if you have not been forewarned about them, you simply have to do a bit of firefighting and try and work it out on the day. If you have ever filmed under sodium lights you'll know exactly what I mean. They are the lamps emitting a very warm color

FIG 3.8
"If you get caught with only one microphone for a walking, talking shot with two guests then position it on the inside lapel and point it in between the two people."

normally found in large industrial units or illuminating roadways. These produce an orangey type of light that many cameras find hard to color balance and some completely refuse to give you a white balance. They don't have the range to include the sodium light's low color temperature. You'll jut see the script "NG" in your viewfinder after pressing the white balance button.

If you do end up shooting in these conditions, try lighting your subject with a normal tungsten lamp and color balance using a white sheet that is lit half by the lamp and half by the sodium lights. The camera will normally balance using this approximation, and any color imbalance can be corrected with a nonlinear edit package.

If this fails use a straw colored gel or 1/2 color temperature orange lighting gel over the lamp, which will warm it up, and then try white balancing again. But try and keep your subject in the video light at all times as this is where the correct color is to be found. If he wanders out of the lamps light, he will become warmer due to the extra amount of sodium light falling on him. The idea here is that your subject will be the correct color in all shots but the background will be

(a)

(b)

FIG 3.9
Dealing with unwanted glare from the sun. "Typical situation of shooting a person through a windshield? The glare is stopping the camera from getting a correct exposure."

left warmer. If you've used the gel method your color balance will be warmer than normal tungsten at 3200° but not as warm as sodium. This halfway compromise will allow you to shoot and get satisfactory results. And if at first your camera refused to balance in the sodium light alone, you've now effectively found a way to keep shooting and get the shots in the camera.

FIG 3.10
"With a flag held in place the shot will be free of glare."

Controlling Glare

When shooting through car windshields or sloped glass you are liable to suffer from glare or reflections (Figure 3.9a). If you need to get a shot of a person in the front seat of a car the chances are that you'll get 50% reflection of the sky and 50% of the person, which makes for an ugly shot. A polarizing filter will help reduce this in some situations but if you don't have one at hand a simple solution exists. Use a flag, black cloth, or piece of black cardboard and get someone to hold it above the area being filmed and just out of shot (Figure 3.9b and 3.10). This will act as a barrier to the light falling onto the glass that is giving you the glare and leaves you free to expose correctly for the subject sitting inside the car. This will normally cure the problem.

CHAPTER 4

High-Definition Shooting

The essence of this book is to keep ideas practical and straightforward so that we can achieve consistent results in shooting, lighting, audio, and all other location video production matters…and enjoy it all.

HD is just a format, albeit a new and a very good one, requiring new cameras and lenses. It shouldn't change the way we approach our day-to-day location shooting or the way we work in any way.

And that's the correct way to look at it.

Over 90% of the practice that we have been through in the book should remain the same even on an HD shoot. If you have achieved a constant and methodical way of shooting, then HD will pose no problem to you. All that remains is to take note of the new functions and aspects that affect your upcoming shoot or production, work out the ones that are important, and build them into your normal routine. What we don't want to do is alter every aspect of our shooting routine that we rely upon when using SD cameras just because it's an HD shoot.

Before I worked on my first 35 mm film shoot, I borrowed a camera and shot lots of tests on the film stock that I knew I would use on the shoot. Simply by using the camera and shooting simple everyday subjects, I soon became familiar with how the final results would appear when processed. If I had my first forthcoming HD shoot in 1 month's time, I would do exactly the same and persuade a facility house into letting me shoot on one of their cameras during downtime until I became used to it. So let's treat HD shooting in a totally objective way.

HD cameras are now well established in their different formats with SONY's HVR-Z1e, which they label as the entry-level HD camera shooting in HDV (High definition vedio). It records pictures at 1080 line resolution and allows for shooting in HDV and DVCAM formats and uses three Clearvid CMOS (Complimentary metal-oxide semi-conductor) sensors instead of CCDs. The advantage here is high sensitivity with low noise, and the camera can also shoot in 25p for a film look. XDCAM HD offers a removable optical disk recording of its HD pictures. You can choose different data rates between 35, 25- and 18 Mbps. One benefit is that this format supports nonlinear file-based workflow.

SONY's HDCAM allows for recording of European or U.S. frame rates by using 1080/50i and 1080/59.94i and the ability to shoot 25p again for a film look (Figure 4.1).

FIG 4.1
"SONY HDCAM."

HDCAM SR, which is SONY's top format, can record RGB of 4:4:4 and component 4:2:2 HDV at 10 bits, so this gives it a resolution of 1920 × 1080.

Panasonic's AG-HPX170 P2 camera uses solid state recording and can shoot both HD and SD with an HD–SDI interface (Figure 4.2). It uses two slots for recording

FIG 4.2
"Panasonic AG-HPX170 P2 video camera."

onto P2 cards and supports 1080p shooting along with others. It can also output the P2 information using USB 2.0 to other computer-based edit systems.

The new concept RED camera, which is capable of a resolution of 4520 × 2540 and aims to be upgradable as technology improvements happen, is pushing the HD boundaries, and Ultra HD is around the corner (Figure 4.3).

The baffling part comes in trying to understand all the HD resolutions and settings and how they will affect shooting, postproduction, and the end result, although in most cases your clients will probably make the decision about which one they want to use, on the basis of where the end product will be postproduced, viewed, or played.

Usefully, if you use the SONY's HVR-Z1e camera to shoot normal SD onto its DVCAM tape, then you get the advantage of excellent pictures partly because of the circuitry of the camera. But just to highlight how important the total workflow of your video productions is, you need to be aware that down-converting would be necessary if you use the camera in HDV mode and then want to end up with an SD end product. So once again you will need to plan and research your shoots to ensure that you have the right kit to produce your end result on the format you or your client wants. The larger cameras shoot full blown HD of 1920 × 1080 resolution.

FIG 4.3
"Redder than a new red thing...The 4K RED camera system."

PROGRESSIVE OR INTERLACED?

Another choice when you come to shoot in an HD is whether to go progressive or interlaced denoted by the letter "p" or "i" at the end of the resolution figures. Interlaced pictures are the way SD cameras have been processing images for many years, and accordingly will get that similar look even on an HD camera. Progressive shots have no fields, as interlaced do; they simply have all the information in one frame and can give a good film look. Additionally, you can also vary the frame rates, but remember to check that your edit system can handle it before shooting the whole project at 24p.

Points to be aware of for camera operators working in progressive are that a 180 degree shutter setting helps to get a good final picture. Many video cameras will default to a shutter of 25th when shooting 25p and this can lead to the picture movement looking slightly "smeared."

Progressive pictures work well when being compressed for transmission. An EBU (European Broadcasting Union) recommendation is for productions to be shot in 1080 25p moving on to 1080 50p in the future when technical improvements allow it to happen.

For the consumer video market, a system called AVCHD now exists. Advanced video codec HD uses mpeg4 compression to produce true HD pictures and it is a 1080i resolution. The cameras are very small, around 500 g (1 lb) in weight, and store the rushes onto hard disks, but as yet the cameras miss out on many primary manual functions that we are used to on pro shooting. But it's simply remarkable that just a small unit can produce such highquality images. Cameras include Panasonic's HDC-SD5 with 3 × 1/16 in. CCDs and SONY's HDR-CX6 with 1/2 × 9 in. CMOS sensors instead of CCDs, costing approximately £800 or £1300 each (Figures 4.4 and 4.5).

FIG 4.4
Panasonic's HDC-SD5 which is an AVCH camera and good for second unit HD location shooting.

Although you are unlikely to use them as a main camera for shooting a whole video, they can produce good pictures, which will blend well with main camera HD shots, and can act as a second camera for pickup shots and effects shots. The rushes are transferred by the use of a USB adapter.

So what does this all mean to us as camera people? The larger 2/3 CCD location HD cameras need HD specific lenses and monitors to give the best results.

FIG 4.5
SONY HDR CX6.
"AVCHD cameras from, good for second unit HD shooting."

So already the budget, whether buying or hiring, is up and you have to have the correct kit which for lenses means that they'll be heavier and costlier (they will probably reduce in price when HD kit is more common), and only a specific HD monitor will give you a good picture to light and work to.

The camera unit itself will also be heavier and use more battery power, although this situation will probably improve as time goes by. I spoke to some cameramen who had used HD cameras over the past year and here are some of their comments. They are not hard and fast rules but firm opinions from people who have worked with the kit and had time to think about the working system as a whole.

- *Treat it carefully*. Lighting your scenes can take more time. Try using soft lights to boost the overall lighting levels especially if you are shooting interiors. Raising the light level helps the picture from looking a bit flat and brings more life to the pictures. In interviews a simple camera top light can give a sparkle to people's eyes. Be prepared to use more lights than you normally would with your SD camera.
- *Because you need a more controlled way of working*, it can get a bit difficult for one-man band shoots, simply because there is more work to do and more things to sort out. It's not a good format for rushing around shoots such as documentary filming when you are following people in an unstructured way. Again this applies to the full blown 2/3 CCD cameras, not to SONY HVR-Z1e and similar cameras that would be ideal for rushing around shoots…if you like rushing around…

- *HD can be unforgiving.* It will show every line and wrinkle on an actor's face so correct makeup is a must on important shoots. And if you are shooting on a purpose built set make sure that it's well constructed. HD will show every crack and split in the scenery. A lot of people use a filter in front of the lens to help actress' faces, such as a pro-mist or similar. But with such a good end recorded picture your options to soften and create effects in postproduction are huge and you are not stuck with the filtered look from the camera. Preshoot tests will be invaluable if you want to try out filters and creative lighting on HD.
- *True HD lenses* are made by Canon, Panavision, Cooke, and Zeiss.
- *It's all down to researching* the workflow from the shoot to the edit on HD; the more work you do before turning over on your shoot, the better your end result will be, and the less problems you'll have to deal with on the shoot and after it. Definitely know you p's from your i's…
- *The viewfinder* can have a flicker effect on some settings, so test your chosen settings out first to get used to the effects.
- *Exposure range is increased.* Because the cameras have such an increased contrast latitude, they can show more detail in dark areas as well as detail in highlight areas and it can at first be confusing on where to set the exposure. Treat it like old-fashioned reversal film and if in doubt, then expose for the highlight areas in the shot.
- *HD brings a host of good options for creating the coveted film look* as your depth of field is quite shallow and the quality is so high. You'll see more detail in the shadows and black areas and also in highlight areas. All this enhances the final picture. On SD you would have to light the darker areas of the scene to bring out any detail and bring down the highlight areas so it doesn't blow too much.
- *Careful focussing of the camera* is also needed with this slender depth of field. A good monitor will be a great asset when shooting in an HD format. TV Logic, Teletest, and some other manufacturers make LCD battery powered HD monitors, which allows the user to pick a part of the picture and zoom in to check focus. Called focus assist, it allows you to check the camera's focus over several parts of the frame you are shooting and will then get a good idea of how sharp or soft you are on that shot or scene, which is essential for shooting on HD cameras.
- *As a tool and format for drama,* the range of different looks you will get from HD makes it unequaled. This is probably the format to make your resume or CV sing…

- *Many drama cameramen will come to HD having shot on film* and I know that some have said they find it harder to get a softer look on HD than on film stock. Another trick is to use only soft light on faces to try and eliminate any blemishes.
- *Many production companies use HD* because they believe it offers "future proofing" and their productions will then have a longer shelf life for future transmissions and future sales.

Although it doesn't affect operation directly, it's worth noting that large TV stations have policies about mixing HD formats with other formats in finished programs. Many will not accept more than 25% of material not shot on HD, and this includes DigiBetacam, HDV, XDCam EX, and super 16 mm film. Cameras that are acceptable for HD filming are SONY HDCAM and Panasonic DVC Pro 100 tape and P2 versions. So if you are producing programs and content on a commission basis, then you'll have to study the small print before you choose your camera combination. When I produced TV shows in the U.K., we had a constant battle with our commissioning editors trying to persuade them to let us use the cameras we knew would be able to handle the shoots best as the TV stations had such a narrow list of formats to choose from.

As you would expect, the cameras have an extensive range of different settings, so it helps to decide beforehand as to which ones you want to work on and the effect you want to achieve. But if you are not completely sure of how to do this in the camera's menus, then leave it to a video engineer to set up. I heard that a good effect can be had with Sony's XDCam using the variable frame rate. A nice subtle slow-motion effect can be had using 32 fps.

Finally it's true to say that the whole topic of HD filming is, at the moment, overcomplicated and this makes it tricky and time consuming to work out exactly how to organize shoots, hire or buy cameras, work out the best way to edit, etc. for projects shot on HD. It is still a young, new format. But as time moves on there will be more hard information about which settings work for certain programming and which don't. And this will lead to more clarity and simpler ways of working for all crews. So if you find yourself scratching your head and looking into the blue sky for inspiration when someone asks you about HD, then don't worry, we're all doing it to some extent.

CHAPTER 5

Location Audio

Location audio breaks down into two aspects for single camera shooting. One when you are working with a sound recordist as a two-man team and the other for when you are a one-man band, coping with camera, lights, and sound on your own (Figure 5.1).

It also affects what equipment can be used as the two-man band sound kit will be considerably more comprehensive than that of a one-man band. But

FIG 5.1 Typical two-man crew location with Nigel Francis doing sound recording on an interview for BBC.

whether you are a single unit or working in a larger crew, the aim for audio is the same, to record the cleanest possible sound in the location that you are shooting in. It's probably true to say that no two locations ever have the same noise characteristics and that each place you'll film in will have its own set of problems to sort out. Ideally you would always have a Sennheiser 416 stick microphone (or similar mic) 4 in. above the subject's head in a soundproof room without air-conditioning or heating, and you'll be using a professional monitoring system…This hardly ever happens…

If you are shooting in a football stadium, such as doing interviews or vox pops even as a game is happening, then you'll have to accept that the ambient noise levels will be quite high, so your challenge is to make sure that the subject's audio is not fighting with other sounds, and it would be pointless stopping each take to wait for silence. Many other types of locations will require a similar compromise or you'll never get the piece recorded.

A standard audio kit for a recordist can be used for many different types of camera from the prosumer versions, through DVCAM, ENG, and up to HDCAM. The recordist's kit is unlikely to vary and will normally consist of an audio mixer such as an SQN 4 into 2 or sound devices 442 with 4 inputs and 4 direct outputs plus left and right outputs and boom pole with Sennheiser 416 or similar with fluffy for reducing wind noise, personal microphones such as SONY ECM 77's, a radio microphone, and possibly a handheld radio along with XLR extension cables and other assorted accessories.

The kit for one-man operation, again which will cope with most types of camera, would be similar to one as in Figure 5.2.

The one man band sound equipment is basically a cut down version of the two man kit including only the essential items, but it copes with 90% of interviews, features, clips, stand-ups, and many other types of filming. I keep the Sennheiser hand-held radio mics in my locker until they are needed but everything else travels with me on a daily basis. The whole kit bag, including spare batteries and cables, weighs in at 3.5 kg (7.8 lb). Of course it all depends on what type of work you are shooting, but I strongly advise that you keep the essential audio kit with you and then take out the other items when needed.

INTERVIEW AUDIO

This section will be useful to those who have just taken up video shooting, students and people transferring from different areas like editing or the production side. It will help you get a feel for the process of getting good audio even as you

FIG 5.2
Typical one-man band audio kit. Hand held cable mic, hand held Sennheiser radio mic plus transmitter pack which takes an ECM (the receiver is built into the camera back) two ECM 77 clip mics, XLR cables and desk top mic stand for press conferences.

film and once again allow you to make up a simple but effective way of working that will cover most types of filming and give good results. If you have more audio recording experience or you come from an audio or sound recording background then you might want to leap ahead in the book.

We'll assume that you are working alone and don't have the luxury of a sound recordist. It might be an obvious observation, but when you arrive at the location, whether it's inside or outside, take time to listen to the surrounding level of noise. Some offices have air-conditioning units that don't sound loud to your ear, but once a microphone is plugged in and is facing up toward them, the volume is quite strong. If your subjects are quiet speakers, you'll then be faced with a situation where their speech is fighting with the air-conditioning's volume and both get recorded onto tape at a similar level. If this happens, try turning the air-conditioning unit off; if it can be controlled locally, move away from the offending noise to a different part of the room or change rooms altogether.

TIP
Never be afraid to listen back to what you have recorded if you think there might have been a problem even if it holds up the shooting schedule for a short while. It's better to spend a few minutes checking than to move on to the next setup and find out later that the audio is not usable.

If your producer or director is not concerned after you have told him that it's very noisy, then give him the headphones so he can hear the noise himself through the camera and then he can make a decision. That way if he decides to go ahead in the noisy area it's his call and you have the benefit of being able to say that you brought it to his attention before shooting. The same will apply if you are outside and affected by consistent noises such as traffic, aircraft, or construction noise.

AUTOMATIC OR MANUAL?

The automatic setting is a safe mode if you don't have time to monitor the sound being recorded, but it will cut the background noise out, which often sounds unrealistic. So manual is the preferred mode. There are times when auto setting will be more useful. A cameraman shooting live events and handholding the camera would probably not have enough hands left to hold a microphone and adjust levels manually, so auto would be a better way to work.

Before recording, try and do a level check with the person speaking at the volume she intends to use when you record. Although guests and interviewees do this simple check at a normal speaking level, it's not unknown for some people to go much quieter or much louder when you turn the camera on, probably because of nerves. Try and get the audio levels to peak at −18 dB on your camera meters when recording.

MICROPHONE CHOICE

The good news is that there are thousands of microphones capable of good audio, and the bad news is that you only need to choose one or two. A gun microphone, Sennheiser 416 or similar, is an industry standard directional microphone. Others are the Rode NTG 2 and Sennheiser ME66/K6n; both can run on their own batteries and do not have to rely on power from the camera. SONY ECM 77 personal/lapel microphones are also used by many pro recordists.

Radio microphones are useful for many types of shoots, one of the benefits being that on busy shooting schedules you can attach them at the start of the day, line them up, and let the subjects do their thing without interruption other than battery changes. They are also good for wide shots when you can't get a boom microphone into the frame without being seen in the camera shot. Make sure you know how to switch channels easily and quickly on your radio microphone in case you are shooting near other crews using the same channel you are.

MICROPHONE POSITIONS

The next choice is how you intend to mic up the guests. If you are outside and your subjects are standing, then you could give the interviewer a handheld microphone, either cabled or radio, and he then has to swing it between himself and the guest as needed. Using a directional gun microphone, you ideally place it close to the subject's mouth but without being in shot. Normally you will have the mic underneath and pointing upward, but if you need a wide shot then try placing it over the top of the subject and just out of frame, if you have a sound man working with you or a microphone stand available. If it's very windy and you have a fluffy cover, use it as this will effectively kill the wind noise and allow the speech to cut through cleanly. If you use this route, then get the interviewer to hold the microphone in position for the guest to talk and you'll soon see if it comes into your widest shot. If so get the interviewer to move it down, you can also use this as a volume test by asking the guest to speak. You can then set your levels on the camera to read around −18 dB, which will give you a good level for recording recorded.

Personal microphones should ideally be placed about 4 in. below the guest's neck but take into account which way the person is looking and talking. If she is looking more toward her left side, then clip the microphone onto her left lapel to get the best audio as the direction of speech will then cover the top of the microphone. If you place it on the other lapel then she will be facing off mic slightly.

COPING WITH WIND

Shooting outside in strong winds often restricts your microphone choice. A gun mic with a large fluffy on is the safest option but be careful that your headphones fit correctly. If they don't you'll also be hearing the sound of the wind howling around them mixed in with your recorded audio, which will make it hard to decide on levels.

PERSONAL MICS AND WIND NOISE

The personal tie microphones are very prone to wind noise as they have such a small surface area, so get hold of some push on wind gags for them, which will reduce this considerably. You'll find that tiny wind gags have a habit of falling off the top of the microphone as they are only a press fit, so drop a little superglue on them and they'll stay on. You can still use them indoors with the wind gags on without compromising the sound (Figure 5.3).

FIG 5.3
Two types of wind gag for SONY ECM personal's, foam top and metal top. Because they are so small it's easy to lose them when you are busy shooting on location unless they are stuck on.

HEADPHONES

Monitoring your audio is of course a must, and choosing a set of headphones that will give you an accurate idea of the microphone's performance while shooting is a priority. Add to this is the fact that headphones need to be comfortable and not too heavy in order to be useful over many days' location shooting; they also need to be robust enough to take the knocks of a regular day's filming, traveling, and repeated packing. Two sets of headphones that pro sound recordists like working with are the Sennheiser HD 25s and the SONY MDR-7506. The HD 25s are closed, dynamic headphones and are quite compact in size and design, light enough for constant use, and made from strong durable materials. They perform well on location and are good in noisy environments (Figure 5.4).

The SONY MDR-7506s are closed, large diaphragm, and foldable. They replaced the SONY MDR-V6s and are again a popular choice for stereo sound monitoring. Both will serve you well over the years. All users of headphones will need to be aware of ongoing noise at work that will affect their health and safety in using this type of kit.

FIG 5.4
Sennheiser HD 25s lightweight, robust, single sided cable and good for location work with a frequency response of 16–22,000 Hz.

TIP
If, like me, you have to do a lot of shoots where you look after the camera, lights, and sound, then you might find this tip helpful. When I'm shooting handheld and trying to monitor the audio, I found that full size headphones always pushed my eye away from the camera viewfinder as there is just not enough room between the side of the camera body and the side of the viewfinder. I now use a pair of Sennheiser OMX-70 stereo earphones for these jobs, which hook over the ear and then you place the earphone into the ear. These stay in place really well – they were made for runners – and don't fall out when you take the camera on and off your shoulder. They also give good audio quality as well (Figure 5.5).

BUZZ TRACKS

A buzz track, or atmosphere track, is a recording of the ambient sound in the place that you are filming in. This can be used in the edit as a bed of sound to create a constant background noise that runs over the edits and smooths the transitions between cuts out.

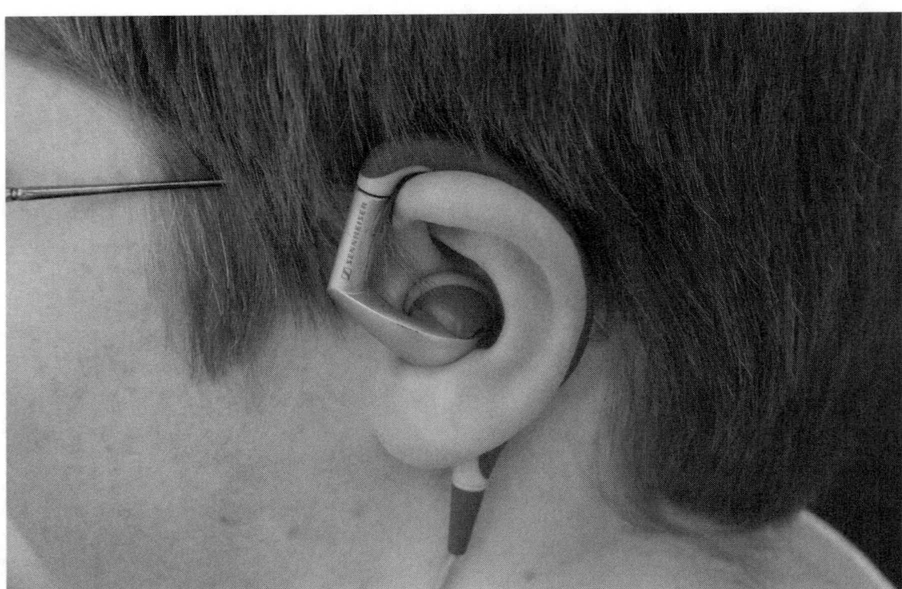

FIG 5.5
OMX-70s clip over your ear for a secure fit and give you room to get your head right next to the camera body when doing handheld camera work with ENG type cameras.

TIP
If you have to film two people walking and talking as a moving interview but only have one radio microphone channel, then think about using this one microphone but cleverly placed to pick up sounds from both people (see Figure 3.7).

VOICE-OVERS ON LOCATION

Many times on shoots you get asked to record the voice-over at the end of the shooting day. But it always seems to work out that there is never enough time for this last job; however, if the producer schedules it into the day, you have to find a way to cope.

Over the many years that I've been filming abroad, we developed a useful method of getting good voice-over audio laid down in many obscure and strange locations. One of the best tricks is to use your car. With the windows wound up, the inside of a car is surprisingly "dead" and, as long as the outside noise is not too intrusive, you can happily record voice-overs of good quality (Figure 5.6).

A quiet hotel bedroom is good; you can deaden the sound of the room even more by hanging the bed linen over windows and doors. In India, when filming on a river bank, we made a makeshift voice-over booth out of our sleeping bags; it

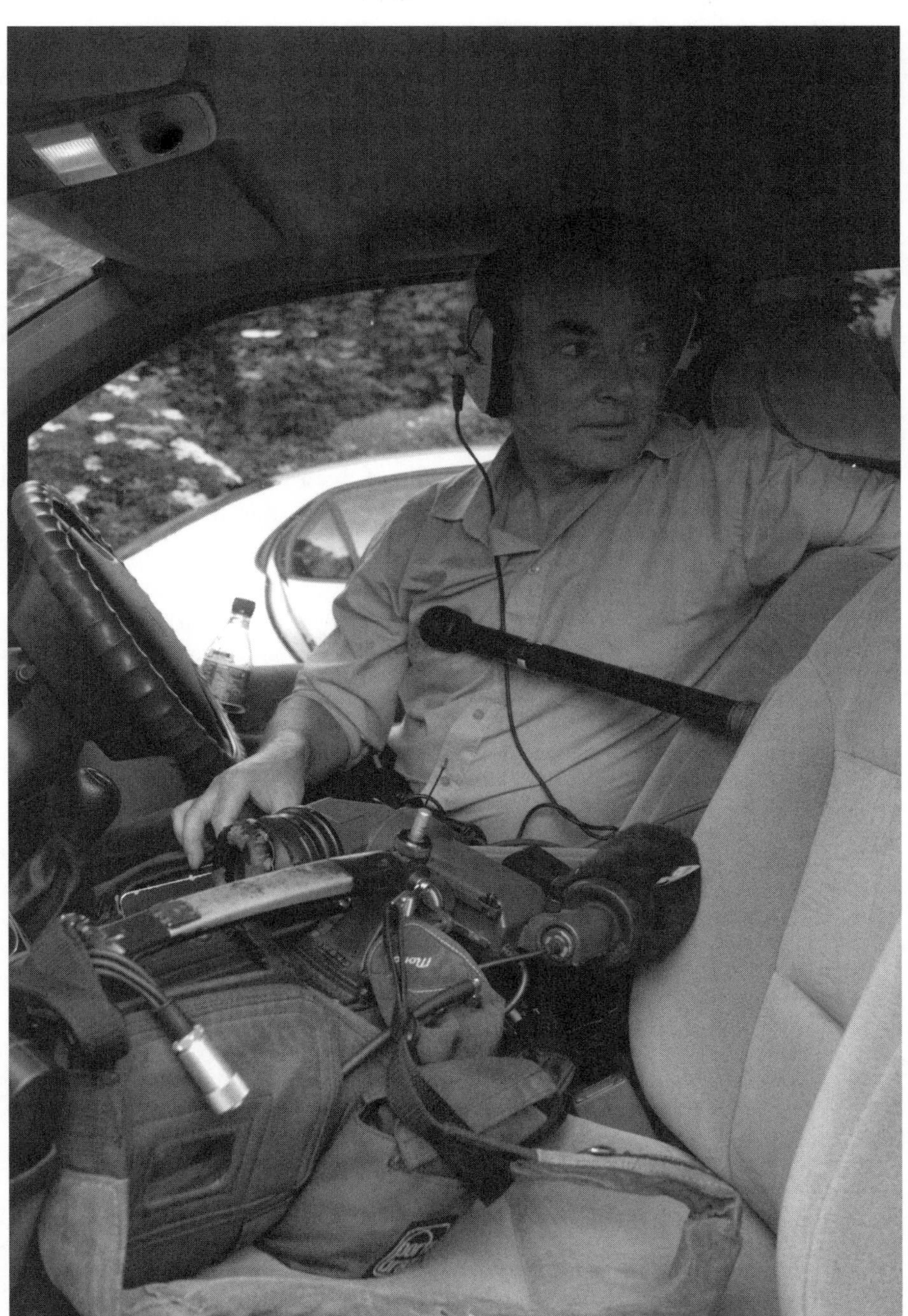

FIG 5.6
Ian Birch uses his crew truck as an effective voice-over booth on location. He mixes the sound straight to the camera and the producer uses the time-code to check that each take is the correct length. You can then drop these audio sections straight into the edit as they will be time-coded on the camera tape.

worked fantastically well. Using the LCD screen on the camera with the time-code display selected, it's possible to get the voice-overs to the exact length needed for the final edit, which is another way of saving time and money.

DIGITIZING AUDIO INTO HARD DISK UNITS

Many stations and TV companies now use server-based audio editing systems. There are a lot of benefits in this approach. You can produce pieces for both radio and TV transmission from the same rushes and you can edit as soon as the rushes have been ingested and the finished piece is given a file or section name, which can then be accessed by other people in different buildings, towns, or even countries. One tip that we found recently while producing a piece might be useful to you. If you take both tracks of audio from the camera into the computer from your rushes you will need to find out if the software package can keep them separate and not mixed together. If, like the audio system we work on, it mixes them together and does not allow you to undo this, then you'll be taking in mixed audio information from both channels 1 and 2. So if, for example, you've laid down the presenter's audio onto track 1 and left track 2 on the camera microphone as a safety, then both will be transferred to the computer and the result will be a strange mix of both microphones, whereas what you actually need is only channel 1. This applies more to audio edit packages, as AVID and Final Cut Pro allow you to choose which tracks you want digitizing.

RADIO TRANSMITTERS NEAR OR ON WATER

Although not essentially a tip for interviews this next one is good for peace of mind when filming near water, especially saltwater (Figure 5.7).

TIP

If you have to film from boats or the water's edge and you are using a radio microphone then beware of getting the transmitters doused with seawater. No matter where you place it on the presenter, usually the back pocket in trousers, there is a good chance that water might get into it, and saltwater and expensive components don't normally mix. Try pushing the transmitter into a condom and then putting it on the presenter, this way even if a stray wave or splash covers him or her then your kit will stand a chance of being saved and be ready for use again.

FIG 5.7
Saltwater will damage electric components in no time at all. Many sound recordists use a simple condom to house the transmitter unit when shooting from boats or near the water's edge just for peace of mind. I always thought they were for safe sex not safe sound.

TIP

If any of your video kit does get splashed with saltwater, turn it off immediately, remove the tape and battery, and wipe it down with clean freshwater. Let it dry out naturally without overheating it and then use a clean cloth on any bare components such as battery contacts.

CHAPTER 6

Interview Shooting Techniques

For most types of TV shows, documentaries, sequences, and corporate videos an interview with a presenter, a guest, or a celebrity will probably need to be shot (Figure 6.1).

FIG 6.1
Crew filming interview.

In fact the humble interview is the bread and butter of most days, shooting, so it's a good place to start and get a few tips on how best to handle different situations. We'll start with some fundamental camera setups and tips for interviews, then move onto a location lighting rig that works for interviews in many situations but that can be adapted to suit different places and different locations.

This lighting setup allows you to use 1–3 video lights, so you can adapt and change as needed. If a lamp breaks during the day or perhaps you can only carry one light with you along with all the other kit you need you'll still be able to get good results by using the setups described here. As no two locations are the same you'll have to adapt these examples to fit your needs, but the general principal should remain the same. There are photos of each change to the setup showing the different effect you'll get while using 1, 2, or 3 lights in normal real-world situations. The main point of this setup is that it will produce good results every time and whether you are shooting a member of the public or Kylie Minogue, this rig works.

The pace of filming today is faster than ever before and because of this it is easy to make mistakes due to rushing. Interviews that are rushed can be a prime source of mistakes. Shooting on location, whether a great outside view or an airy modern office, allows you to get away from a studio and use different interesting backgrounds and bring some creativity to what is a staple part of virtually every TV show or video production in the world. As I've mentioned before you will need to develop a consistent way of shooting these interviews in order to cope with a busy day's filming. Break your technique down to the simplest few stages that produce consistently good results. After doing this you can move onto increasingly creative interview techniques and make the production values higher without compromising your speed of working.

For people who are new to location shooting on single camera, go through the first setup points I make here, and for others who have already got a good grasp of the fundamentals, move ahead to the more advanced steps. Just before we look at the lighting set-ups it's worthwhile checking the right way of setting up the camera for interviews, stand-ups and pieces to camera.

SETTING UP CAMERA HEIGHT

This might seem a very obvious point but you'd be surprised at how important it can be when shooting on single camera and especially when you come to film any reverse shots to help your edit.

In general I'm sure you have all been taught to set the camera lens height at the eyeline height of the presenter or questioner you are working with and who is

standing next to your camera. This means that as the subject you are filming looks at the presenter's eyes while he speaks this eyeline is also correct for the camera height as both are lined up (Figure 6.2). If you've not been taught this then consider it now done.

FIG 6.2
This camera is the right height for shooting as the eyeline of the subject will not appear too low or too high in the shot.

But there are times when you need to relax this rule, especially if you are going to be filming the reverse questions after the main interview. First you might be after a certain program style or effect in which the camera looks up or down at the subject, in which case go ahead; all you have to worry about is matching the shot sizes and camera height when you come to film the opposite angle. See the section "Shot Sizes" later in this chapter.

At other times you might be working with a tall presenter who has a short guest, or the other way around. Let's take the case of a tall presenter and a shorter guest. Choose a camera height about 1 foot lower than your presenter's eyes (Figure 6.3).

This won't be too noticeable in the final shot and will help you get a more pleasing shot of the guest. Sometimes when the camera looks down on a subject from too high a position, the person's neck seems to be joined to his shoulders, which is very unflattering, and the background becomes dull as it can feature more ground than landscape.

FIG 6.3
Camera is 1 foot below the tall interviewers eye height and gives a good compromise for shooting two guests when they are very different heights.

This also means that when you come to shoot the other way for the interviewer's shots, you can then choose a camera height that corresponds to the first set of shots and is not too low (as you will position the camera about 1 foot higher than the guest's eyeline) and has an excess of sky in it. By doing this you will lessen the impression that one person is much taller than the other as the backgrounds will be similar, and again, this will look better when the two angles are cut together in the final edit.

DISTANCE FROM SUBJECT TO LENS

When we are expected to film interviews quickly this point can be overlooked and result in some really bad shots.

I use an Ikegami HL DV7w DVCAM with a Canon 9 × 5.2 lens. This lens is now quite old but it is a truly great lens with a useful wide angle of view on its widest zoom position, but it also allows me to flip in a 2× lens converter to double the tight end when needed. With this combination, a nice wide angle and an OK tight lens, I can shoot a variety of cutaway shots for the editor to choose from, which include wide shots with lots of foreground and tight shots with compressed foregrounds for contrast. This all makes for interesting footage and proves yet again that a wise choice of lens will last many years and provide good service.

But I shoot a lot of interviews with older politicians, both men and women, in Westminster, and on busy days it's all too easy for the journalist asking the questions to stand right next to the camera, which then brings the guest far too close to my lens. This forces me onto the wider end of the lens and provides an extremely unflattering end shot. To add to the problems, if the guest has receding hair and a double chin, the result becomes similar to using a fish-eye lens, overemphasized and "barrel"-like. And if you are even a little bit too low with the camera height the effect is worse. This has to be avoided at all costs but when you are asked to film quickly it's easily done.

Always try and get the camera away from your interviewee. Ask the presenter to take two or three steps away from the lens and this will push the guest about four or five steps away from the lens, so you'll be able to zoom in slightly as the guest is now approximately 4 m away, and the end shot will be slightly compressed and less likely to have any exaggerated wide-angle looks to it (Figure 6.4). It will also help to throw the background slightly out of focus, especially if you can work on a wider f-stop.

FIG 6.4
Camera is a good distance from the subject, about 2–3 m away. The operator will have to zoom in slightly and so the lens angle will be more flattering to the subjects face and this will also help give a softer background making the subject stand out more.

If you have an old 35 mm still camera look at the effect given by the 80 and 100 mm prime lenses. These were taken as industry standard "portrait" lenses as they provided the correct look and feel for people's faces. Try and re-create this in your video work; it's a classic look that will always work and always give good results.

If youir interviewers always position themselves right next to the camera out of habit then take a little time to explain that you want them a few steps away and that it will be a better shot for the final edit. Most people are pleased to hear the reasons for this simple procedure and it also reinforces the fact that you are thinking about the final result, which is good for them to know. If, after you've gone through this with them they still stand right next to you and the camera, consider changing your aftershave or perfume as it's probably too nice.

ADD SOME SHALLOW DEPTH OF FOCUS

So you've got your subject correctly positioned, the camera at the right height, and a pleasant background to shoot against; what else is there to think about?

Most video cameras now produce pictures that are sharp from the foreground to the background. This is partly to do with the small CCD chip sizes that are being used in camera production today. However, the end result is that when you are out shooting, this constant sharp image can make shots look similar unless you can find a way of making them more varied. And a variety of shots with different sizes, angles, and depths of field is what you want to aim to provide as these elements will make your rushes stand out from the crowd and will add further interest in the final program.

If you consider that a film camera and lens can work to a focus position with only a few inches separating the sharp area to the out of focus area, that's a major difference to our video cameras. It's also a major factor as to why video cameras find it hard to produce the "film look."

But there are a few things we can do to try and get a narrower depth of field for these interviews and cutaways that will help bring the subject away from the background slightly and give the effect of a narrow depth of field. Zooming in on the lens or the camera positioned away from the subject also helps. Now we have to get the camera working at a wider aperture as this will again assist in throwing the background out of focus (Figure 6.5).

If your camera has an internal neutral density (ND) filter you can dial this in, if there is enough light available to do so. It will force the camera to work at a wider f-stop. If the day is truly very bright think about putting the 2× lens converter in (assuming the camera has one) as this will again allow you to open up another one or two stops. It adds another glass element in front of the camera's

FIG 6.5
With video cameras using ever-smaller CCDs, it gets more difficult to achieve a shallow depth of focus and therefore make the subject stand out more in the frame. Use a wide f-stop, move the camera away, and zoom in to get this pleasant effect.

CCDs making the picture darker until you open the iris more. Now your camera should be on a wide aperture; you've got some distance between you and the subject and the ND filter is helping as well. So you should be seeing the background looking softer with this narrowing depth of field and the subject should be taking priority in the frame.

It's a good technique to try outside on location.

TIP
If you regularly use a SONY HVR-Z1e or similar camera then using the above techniques to get a shallow depth of field will really help your footage. These cameras can produce shots in which the person in the foreground appears to be out of focus compared to the background in certain circumstances, especially when the background object has sharply defined horizontals and verticals, such as an office block or a church. The circuitry keeps these objects pin-sharp, which appears to push the person in the foreground out of focus. Always use manual focus in these situations, never auto as the camera is likely to "hunt" for focus on the sharp background object.

If your camera system doesn't have internal ND filters think about purchasing a set. They can be bought as stand-alone filters in sizes that will cover the front element of your lens and a set of 0.3, 0.6, and 0.9 NDs will give you a good range to work with and cover most levels of brightness. The 0.3 ND filter will reduce the light by one stop and the 0.9 ND filter by three stops. The filters simply drop into a matt box hung on the front of the camera.

If your video camera is without an internal lens extender you can also buy these from video accessory shops; again, it's a worthwhile investment as it will add to the range of shots you can provide.

SHOT SIZES

At this point it's worth going over different shot sizes. Partly because on single camera shooting there will be times when you will need to describe to other people working with you verbally what type and size of shot you are going to film and also because editors, directors, and producers will expect you to know these sizes and the abbreviated terms for them as they will use them to explain what is wanted from the shoot before you start filming. You also need to know these terms when you film two camera sequences and both cameramen need to describe what shot sizes they will be shooting on the different subjects, or producers and directors want to get both cameras on the same size shot for a neat edit.

VWS	Very wide shot. Where the person/people in the shot are framed with a lot of air in the top and bottom of frame.
WS	Wide shot. Half the size of the above shot.
LS	Long shot. Where a person is framed top to bottom and there is a small amount of air left between the head and the top of the frame and the feet and the bottom on the frame.
MS	Mid-shot. Where the person is framed from the top of the head (with a small gap to the top of frame) to the waistline or belly button.
MCU	Medium close-up. Where the person is framed from the top of the head down to the chest or breast line. You can also have a "loose" MCU, which is slightly wider, and a tight MCU, which is slightly tighter.
CU	Close-up. From the hairline of a person's head to just below the chin.
BCU	Big close-up. Eyes and mouth...very dramatic.

BACKGROUNDS MATTER

When choosing the best position to set up for your interviews on location it's worthwhile thinking about how the background will affect the shot and also the subject matter. If, for example, you are shooting a presenter who is talking about the effects of busy roads and pollution then shooting the piece next to a noisy, busy road would be quite relevant and the sound of the road would be in context with the topic. But if the subject matter is not that specific and you need to record a lengthy interview in this location, then the road noise in the background will become tiresome as you fight the audio level of the traffic and the constant movement of the vehicles will take the viewer's attention away from the subject being discussed.

Interior locations can also have some distracting backgrounds best avoided, like elevators and busy corridors. When you come to edit the final piece, these ever-changing backgrounds will make it hard to get clean edits without people jumping in and out of frame as they constantly change position in the shot. This will be a major headache if you are filming a long interview but probably acceptable if it's a short clip.

Lastly, beware of placing your subject in front of buildings with towers, spires, and masts as it's all too easy to have one of these large, tall objects growing out of your subject's head on the final recording when you are concentrating on the audio at the time. No one ever looks best with a telegraph pole growing out of one's head…

TIP

When you film inside a building run by other people always make sure you use lightweight rubber mats or security tape to cover any cables that might trail across doorways or walkways, and use an RCD (residual current device) (see Figure 15.2, Chapter 15) between your film lights and the mains power. This is a small, low-cost item that will disconnect a circuit whenever it finds that the current flow is unbalanced. It assumes this as a leak and clicks off. If you do bring in multiple film lights for shooting, it's a good idea to talk to the house electricians before you arrive. They'll be able to help; possibly they can supply mats and extension cables for you to use and will also highlight any mains plugs and circuits that you cannot use, like those dedicated to computer networks.

So we've gone through some fundamental setting up tips and techniques that always work for interviewing people on location.

Audio recording tips and techniques for interviews on location are covered in Chapter 5.

While you've been getting the camera in the right position and checking for a good background plus sorting out the sound, you've obviously been thinking about how the light will fall on your subject. Haven't you?…Of course you have…

As location lighting is a vast topic most of it will be dealt with in Chapters 9–11, but we'll make a start here on a few simple rigs that work time and again for video shooting of interviews in different locations. You can use them in many places, varying them slightly, but they work nine out of ten times. Again the emphasis is on having a consistent way of working and some routine/normal setups that you can rely upon to deliver the results on even the hardest day, and you'll know that the rushes will look fine in the edit suite.

GENERAL INTERIOR INTERVIEW SETUP

Most interior locations that you use for filming your interviews will have some form of natural light, either from daylight coming into the room through windows or from the bulbs and lamps that are installed in the room. So you can choose to use this existing lighting or close it out and start from scratch, as if you are in a studio.

So if you have a lot of time and the right number of video lamps available to you, then you can shut it all out and build up your lighting just as you want it, but in reality the pressure to get scenes filmed quickly and then move on will probably dictate that you use at least some of the available light and simply add your own to give it the look you want.

In fact, most interior setups and scenes can be approached this way and unless the existing room lighting is really dreadful, our job is to supplement it and shape it with our shooting lights.

We'll assume that your producer is chomping at the bit, the guest only has half an hour of free time, and the next setup is in a taxi ride across the town in 1 hour's time (because this seems to be the way my filming days always go…) but that you all want to get a good-looking interview in the can and not worry about it after you've moved on. It can be used for a guest who is sitting or standing. In "real-world" location shooting situations, problems have to be solved quickly and effectively, so if you are short of time or short of lights or one of your lights has broken down, you can adapt this to work with 1–3 lights and it will create good results in most locations.

Figure 6.6 is a shot of the location we will be shooting in showing the natural light falling into the area before we turn on the film lamps.

FIG 6.6
Here's the location showing the natural light coming in and bouncing around the shooting area before the video lights are switched on.

Windows to the right of the camera let in a fair amount of light and illuminate the general area while the neutral colored walls to the left of frame will allow some of this natural light to bounce back and act as fill-in light to fall on our subject as long as we don't over light him with our key lamp. If we did use a powerful key light, then this useful fill-in daylight will be overpowered and will not register in the shot, and I'm a firm believer in keeping lighting natural and subtle so our video lights will not be so bright as to lose the effect of this natural light, and we'll get the benefit of working at a wide f-stop, which will help give us a shallow depth of field for the shot. We'll also let the daylight help us fill in around the guest and light any background naturally.

If you do decide to shut out all the daylight you'll have to light the surrounding area as well as your subject, which will take more time and more lamps.

However, if you wanted a final look that needed the subject to stand out against the background, then losing all the natural light and using only the video lamps would be the best way to do it.

As I've used the lights at low level, the picture shows (see Figure 6.7) the effect of the soft fill light from the wall. If I had my lights at a higher power output,

FIG 6.7
Three lights used, 150 Arri is the key light working at 75% output, 150 watt Dedo is the back light at 50% output and 20 watt fill light on top of the camera, plus ½ blue gels on them. All are direct, hard light and on full flood positions. The key light comes from the right of camera to simulate the daylight. Because I've kept the video light levels low the daylight is reflected off the wall to the left of this picture and adding some soft fill light to the subject.

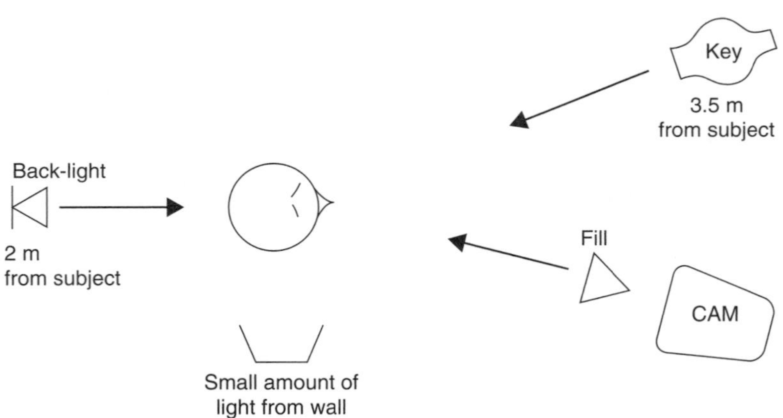

FIG 6.8
Here's the plot of the lamps showing distance from the subject and angle from the camera.

the key light on the right of camera, it will place a harder shadow on the opposite side of the guest's face (the right side), which is nearest or toward the camera and which is a classic lighting setup, giving you a balanced feel to the face and the shot. You'll see this "shadow to camera" style in many films, commercials, and top-end TV shows because it works well in so many different situations. If you are new to lighting then practice it until you get a good result.

The fill light is the on-camera PAG light, which will also give a sparkle to the guest's eyes because it is lower in height than the key and roughly at the guest's eye height. It will help soften any shadows on the face and neck area but not interfere with the key light's work. It is at least half the power of the key light.

Lastly a backlight is used again at about 50% power in relation to the key light. This backlight is on a dimmer, so we can control its intensity. You can control the level with ND gels clipped onto the barn doors but a dimmer is easier and allows for more subtle work.

TIP
These on-camera lamps used to be called "bashers," and they do give a nice effect to people's eyes. If you want to get the best effect of this light then sometimes the light needs positioning slightly off camera and toward the key light. It all depends on your subject.

As we have the window in the right side of the shot I've allowed it to be a bit brighter than the other parts of the shot to give some interest to the shot.

If you want to bring the brightness level of the window down you have two choices: use more light or put ND gel over the window.

If your guest has a bald head then you'll only need a very small amount of backlight or you'll end up with a hot spot on the head. If your guest has light gray or white hair, you'll again have to keep the light at a fairly low intensity, but someone with brown or black hair will be able to take more light.

This setup works time and again and gives good results in many different kinds of locations.

FIG 6.9
So if you only have two lights you can use a key and backlight giving you an effect similar to this picture.

You can change and adapt the three light rig. If you only have two lights then try using a key and backlight as seen in Figure 6.9. The look is a bit 'harder' on the face but still gives a good feel to the subject.

When you have a key light and no backlight, keep the key light at a very low level so that the small amount of daylight bouncing off the side walls can act as a fill light and you'll still get a usable picture. The key here is to work at low light levels and not use an overbright key light.

Finally Figure 6.10 shows the same setup but with only a key light. Used properly you will still get a good effect, but keep the lamp levels low. I've angled a wall light to illuminate the plant behind Adrian's head which helps make him stand out more in the frame. Because the first lighting rig (Figure 6.7) with three video lights had them placed correctly then the next two setups (Figures 6.9 and 6.10), using only two and then one light, keeps the lamps in the same position.

Keep it subtle and always check how the light is falling and working on the subject's face. Everybody's face is different, so you'll need to adapt the light's position and height to get the best picture.

One last tip that will help you save time and effort. On the rig we've been discussing previously there is a good chance that you will need to film a wide two shot to help the editor get in and out of clips and also the presenter's questions.

FIG 6.10
Adrian lit with only the key light and no back light or fill light.

By pulling your camera back you will get a good wide shot that does not show the presenter's lips moving and will be ideal for the purpose needed. However, if you leave the lights positioned as they are the presenter will be much darker than the guest as the rig is only lighting the guest. But if you have used three lights simply pull back the key light so it acts as a backlight on the presenter, but still illuminates the guest. Then spot the existing backlight up onto the presenter's face and you now have a setup that looks balanced for both of them and will have taken only a few minutes to prepare and saves you taking down the existing lights and changing their positions around.

This should also help you if you need to turn the camera noddies a round (for reverse shots) and shoot the presenter for his questions and noddies or reaction shots.

I hope I have introduced you to a lighting setup for location interviews that is truly practical and adaptable and that will work for the "real-world" shooting that you do. The basic principle of this is that you can use it to achieve a good shot with very little time spent rigging up the lights. You can choose to film either with all the available light or just your film lights. If you only have one or two lamps at your disposal or a few bulbs break during the day and you are forced to shoot with less lights simply use a bit more ambient light from the windows as I have illustrated in Figures 6.9 and 6.10 and position the lamps

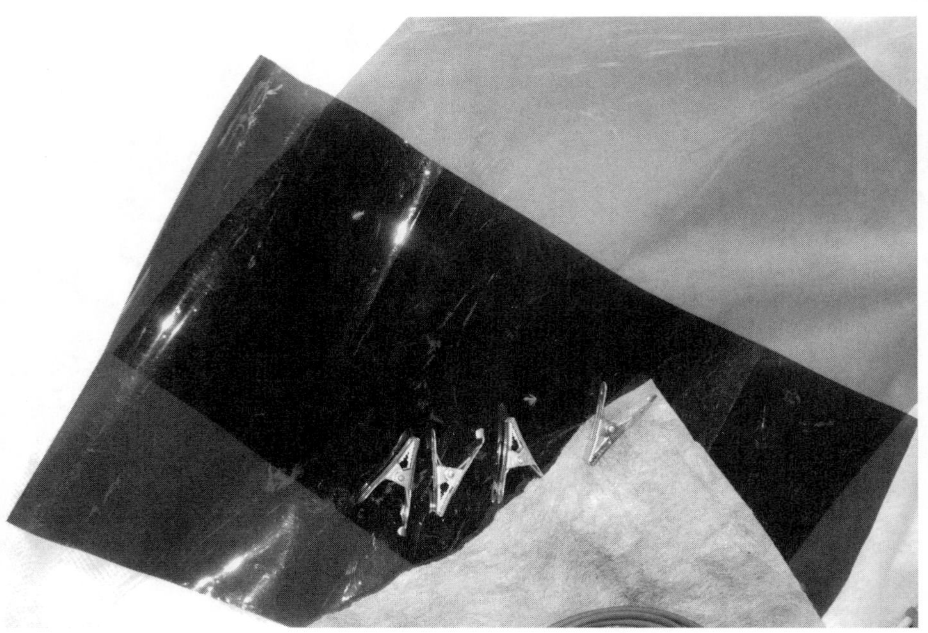

FIG 6.11
To save carrying loads of different lighting correction gels, just take one or two sheets of 1/2 blue gel and 1/2 CTO (color temperature orange). If you have a scene that needs a full blue gel putting on the lights then simply fold over the 1/2 blue gel and it will act as a full blue and correct your tungsten light to 5600 K. The same can be done with the 1/2 CTO and you use this on a daylight-based light such as an Hydrargyrum Medium Arc-iodide (HMI) and the gel will then correct this to tungsten 3200 K." Add a sheet of 0.3 ND and a sheet of trace or spun to your kit bag and you'll be able to cope with many different lighting set-ups.

you have left as I have illustrated in Figure 6.11. If you have better lights with flags and gobos at your disposal you will get better production values but the essence is that this simple rig will allow you to change it to your needs and it will work with celebs, stars, politicians, etc.

TIP

After lighting a scene always sit or stand in the position that you want the subject to be. If the lighting feels uncomfortable to you it will to them also; perhaps you've got the lamps too close to the subject or possibly the light is in full spot and not full flood mode. Comfortable lighting helps guests relax, which means you'll get a better interview from them.

Finally, try and run the lights on the full flood position rather than the 'spot' position unless you really need that extra intensity but have not got a larger wattage lamp with you to use.

CHAPTER 7

Shooting Sequences

In Chapter 6, we looked at tips and techniques for shooting interviews on location. Another large part of everyday shooting is creating shots for good-looking sequences and packages that can edit together well and tell the story in pictures. Many readers will probably know about this topic, but if you are coming from a journalistic background or perhaps studying film and video, or possibly you are a sound engineer who is changing to cameras, then this chapter will give you the basics about shooting sequences and the confidence to do a good creative job on your next shoot.

Now to avoid any doubt when I talk about a sequence I mean any duration of finished video and audio, short or long, that has to be edited together from separate shots to make a polished, coherent final cut. There are bound to be many different names for exactly the same thing, but it doesn't matter what it's called; it only matters that you know how to shoot it correctly. Don't let people baffle you with jargon.

FIRSTLY, WHERE WOULD SEQUENCES BE USED?

Just about every type of TV show or video production utilizes a version of a sequence. Current affairs shows use them to explain topical stories. News shows use them to set up interviews and pieces to camera. Soap operas use a kind of sequence to start off storylines and explain plots, etc. They are a good, clear way of explaining to the viewer what it's about and why it's happening before moving on to the next part of the story, and a well-made sequence leaves the viewer knowing more about the topic than before seeing it. A badly made sequence leaves the viewer knowing very little more or wondering what it's all about, and the camera shots have to play their part in telling this story.

WHAT IS THE BEST WAY TO SHOOT A SEQUENCE?

Well it depends on what it's for and who is producing it, but there are a few guidelines that we can use to ensure that our shots work and the editor has the right rushes to work with in the edit. Don't think of them as rigid rules; use them as a starting plan and then add your own creativity to the job you are doing. But most importantly, when you are shooting them always ask yourself if the shots will edit and how well they will edit. If you feel that the shots won't cut while filming then stop and think again, because you're probably right. This way you will be actively helping the sequence to cut and working at the right shots instead of just shooting shots that might work.

WHY DO WE NEED SEPARATE TAKES OF THE SAME ACTION FROM DIFFERENT ANGLES?

Most sequences rely on a set of actions from your guests or subjects. If you only shoot from one angle then the viewer will only see a limited amount of what is happening. Depending on what movements are being filmed, this one angle might not be the best place to view all the action from, and you might miss some important information about the scene if you only rely on this single viewpoint. Different angles allow the viewers to see more, and the more they see the more they understand what is going on. Different camera angles like low shots and high shots will help this. Editors also use the different takes and angles to get good clean cuts in and out of the action. Another point to bear in mind is how you feel about what is happening in front of the camera. If you have shot the scene from one angle but are left with a nagging doubt that it's not telling the whole story then think about using another angle or position to let the viewers know precisely what's going on, and this will reinforce the message that is coming across from the sequence.

A good example would be shooting a simple knot, perhaps one used for tying a hook onto a fishing line or a knot used for tying a boat to a mooring. When you look through the action with your eye it might seem that the one angle works fine for the whole process, but through the lens there will be times when you won't see some of the action because the knot tyer's fingers will obscure an important movement for a short while. This is what I mean by a "slight nagging doubt" – you feel it's not quite all there yet. If you then add a couple of different angles, perhaps ones a lot tighter than the first shot, then in the edit the story of this simple knot tying will become much clearer and make it a more polished piece of video. And if you know that the shots have got the message across, then nine out of ten times the viewer will think this as well. Finally, don't forget to grab a couple of tight shots of the knot tyer's face (without his/her hands in frame), so you can shorten the piece as needed in the edit.

WHY USE DIFFERENT SIZED SHOTS?

We need to shoot different sized shots so that the editor can again make neat edits into the live action. If you only shoot wide shots the editor would have a difficult job cutting them together. Tight shots help in editing as well as give a method to shorten a piece of dialog and move onto a different piece that might come from another take. Also, different sized shots add visual variety for the viewer and help tell the story.

DO I NEED TO SHOOT MULTIPLE WIDE SHOTS?

Normally the answer would be no, unless parts of the action are obscured from different angles, or a different part of the background tells the viewer more of the story. So if you do shoot more than one wide shot, always shoot some tighter shots to edit the piece with, or you'll end up with a jump cut.

HOW DO I KNOW MY SHOTS WILL EDIT?

Think like an editor. If you can't see how the shots will cut together through the viewfinder the editor probably won't be able to do it either. Shoot a master wide shot, then do two more versions of the same action, one tighter and the last one a close-up. This way the same action is replicated three times but shot with different sizes that should all edit together and avoid any nasty jump cuts. This allows the editor to have more than one option when he's cutting. This process is useful if the script or story changes between shooting and editing and has to be altered in the edit. For safety always hold your shots for 5–10 seconds longer than you think you should, just in case the editor needs to add longer narration to the final cut.

DO I NEED THE AUDIO TO BE EXACTLY THE SAME ON EVERY DIFFERENT TAKE?

Normally no. But try and get the audio to be similar on every take. As long as you have some takes that do not show people's mouths moving, the editor can lay down a master track with the dialog he wants to use (from your first master wide shot) and then use your other takes to cut different shots in without using the audio from these shots. That's why good cutaways and a variety of different shots always help in the edit.

WHAT CUTAWAYS DO I NEED?

The million dollar question...You need the right ones.

Look at Chapter 12 about the black art of shooting cutaways. A good tip was given to me by Ian Wagdin, who shoots and edits. If in doubt rely on the "4 shot sequence," remembered as close-up of the hands, close-up of the face, point of view shot, and a wide shot. You can adapt these for most shoots but the joy of this simple formula is that it's almost always guaranteed to cut together into a sequence and gives the editor the option of changing the shots around so he can get in and out of shots at the point he needs, and to match any audio/narration.

HOW MUCH TAPE/FOOTAGE SHOULD I SHOOT?

The second million dollar question...Depends on the length of the end piece, really, and how complicated the live action is on your master shot. It also depends on whether you intend to use lots of shortcuts when you'll definitely need a lot of shots to choose from. If you are new to video camera work, then always shoot more than you think you might need. Then talk to the editor after he's cut the piece and ask which shots worked and which didn't. Even better, talk to the editor before you shoot the piece and make a wish list of shots that you both want. After a while you'll get to know how many shots are worth shooting.

I'll end this chapter by going through a simple sequence to show how it can be covered.

The story is about how expensive fresh fruits are to buy in the stores. The big supermarkets have put the blame on the suppliers saying that they have all gotten together and raised the price of some fruits; strawberries, in particular, have gone up by 45%. You are sent to a strawberry farm to shoot an interview with the owner, some live action of the fruits being picked, and a piece to camera with the journalist to end the story, which is to be 2 minutes long.

When you arrive, the journalist goes to talk to the owner and arrange the contents of the interview. You then make a start by shooting some exteriors of the farm, wide shots of the strawberry fields, and tight shots of strawberries on the plants. You keep the camera microphone switched on to record the atmosphere of each area you shoot in.

The interview is shot using the fields behind the interviewee and interviewer as a background, and you can see people picking the fruit in the distance. You shoot three setup shots of the owner talking to his staff, all with different sized shots. Then you line up on a mid-shot of the owner ready for his first answer, and while the second question is being asked you zoom into an MCU and hold this frame for the rest of the interview. After the chat has finished you then shoot a wide two shot from slightly behind the interviewer's shoulder and then some reverse shots of the interviewer along with a few questions and a few reaction shots. One last very wide two shot with a pleasant tree in the foreground completes that section and you are happy that it will edit OK.

Down in the strawberry field two pickers walk side by side through the fruits, picking them and placing them in baskets, talking to each other about the fruits as they go. You shoot a master wide shot of this action, hopefully with a bit of tree or bush in the foreground to give some added interest, and take audio from a radio microphone. You let them walk out of the frame at the end of the take and hold the shot for 10 seconds after they have gone so that the editor can use a slow mix if he needs to. They repeat the action and use similar words on both the mid-shots while you walk back with the camera following them and then shoot close-ups of hands picking fruit and placing it into the basket, and then close-ups of faces, talking and listening. An over-the-shoulder shot of the picker would edit well and complete a good set of shots.

You shoot the presenter's piece to camera in a different location and you do it twice with different backgrounds. Finally you record the voice-over of the script in the hire car, which can be used by the editor to cut the piece, and if it needs changing this can be done in the edit. If for any reason the journalist cannot make the edit the editor can complete the edit using this voice-over you have recorded on location.

So with a bit of luck you have covered the story well, given the editor a choice of shots to use, and got the live action section that tells the story perfectly. Job done....

CHAPTER 8 Shooting for the Edit

SINGLE CAMERA TECHNIQUES FOR MAKING THE EDIT GO SMOOTHLY

Even the best shots in the world will end up on the cutting room floor if they are too short for the editor to use, have a wobble or camera shake in the middle, have dodgy audio, or simply have untidy starts and ends. When filming single camera location items, we need to give the editor footage that can be used in many different ways in case he has to change the way a piece is cut or alter the duration of entire sections.

Let's say you are shooting an intro shot of a lovely old building in warm summer sunshine in order to set up an interview in which the presenter discusses the building.

You decide to pan across the building to show its entire length. You roll tape and start panning straightaway; 15 seconds later you reach the end of the building and stop tape.

When the editor looks at the shot he'll probably want to lay the presenter's interview audio under this setup shot before cutting to the presenter himself, so he'll need a shot that is of the right length or time for this purpose and we'll assume that he needs 10 seconds to do this. The shot we have given him starts panning straightaway and this recorded shot ends as soon as the camera reaches the end of the building. The editor has no choice but to choose either the start of the shot and come out 10 seconds later or use the final

10 seconds of the shot, ending when the camera stops abruptly. Already he has only two choices, and as the camera started the pan without holding a steady frame and ended the shot without a hold then the edit is going to look very untidy. Even if the editor wants to mix in and out he's got very few frames of a steady shot to do so. Even worse, there are no steady frames at the start and finish and if the editor needs to shorten the setup in order to match the presenter's words, he has to use the moving shots as there are no other static shots to choose from. And if there is a camera shake or wobble in the pan then again it's an added problem.

To make sure that we shoot to cover all possible edit problems it's best to develop a consistent way of shooting these setups and cutaways.

1. Always roll tape for at least 5 seconds before you start your shot and always put down bars on a new tape for at least 10 seconds. This gets the tape in the cassette away from the start position where there could be problems.
2. Referring to our example above shoot 10 seconds of a steady shot (of our old building) before starting your pan.
3. At the end of the pan hold the shot steady for a further 10 seconds before cutting tape.
4. If you had any shake or wobble during the pan then do the whole thing again.

This way the editor can now choose to:

a. Use the first steady shot only.
b. Use the end steady shot only or use both shots cut together.
c. Use only the pan, but he can now choose to come to the shot before the camera starts panning or let the camera stop at the end of the pan and hold a few steady frames before cutting away.
d. Use the pan with mixes into or out of the steady shots at the start and end in order to make a tighter edit.
e. Most importantly we have now given him enough choice and variety of shots so he can change the pictures to fit the incoming audio and he is in a position to change the way the sequence is cut if he needs to. If the building you are shooting has interesting details visible then shoot a few very tight shots of this for good measure.

And if he needs to come back to a shot of the building at the end of the edited piece he'll be able to choose a fresh shot rather then reuse a shot from the starting setup he has already edited. And we have made good use of the one shot we did. If you are pushed for time and simply can't do any more cutaways then you have probably covered most problems that the editor may have to deal with by using the technique above.

The old film cameramen used to say "At the end of a shot keep filming for 10 seconds longer than you feel you should."

EDIT YOUR OWN RUSHES...AT LEAST ONCE

If you have never edited your own footage you've missed out on a real treat, possibly...My first job as a director was called "Go Fishing," an international travel and fishing series, and we were filming in the Northwest Territories of Canada trying to catch massive lake trout. I was also the cameraman. It's true to say that I learned more from that one shoot than any other shoot previously but it was a hard lesson to learn. When we eventually came to view the rushes some weeks later and start the off-line edit it soon turned out that I had committed the major sin of location shooting, and there were not enough cutaways. The video editor gave me a very hard time, which I've never forgotten, but I've never made the same mistake again, so I guess I learned what to do.

VIDEO EDITOR'S FORUM

Location shooters can learn lots from video editors who are normally straightforward folks, to the point of being blunt, when rushes come in that are difficult to edit. I asked two well-known and respected location shoot/editors from BBC Wales, Graham Meggit and Rob Selex, to list the problems they face with rushes and what the major mistakes were that they came across.

- *Not white balancing*. Although a bad white balance can be mostly saved in AVID.
- *After framing a shot lots of people expose* for the whole scene rather than the face or subject so the subject is left either too dark or overexposed...A top light would be very helpful to balance things out.
- *Not enough variety* of shots to make a sequence work. Lots of people shoot only mid-shots. Think variety...long shots, mid-shots, and tight shots for everything. They need to think about the end sequence and how it can be made interesting.
- *Audio can be just awful sometimes,* said Graham...overmodulated (too loud), basically from radio mics that are not correctly adjusted. Leaving the gain to look after itself is another mistake.
- *A great lack of people using manual controls* on the camera, mostly relying on auto settings for video and audio. If you've been given a video camera

to use it's tempting to leave it on auto settings and not worry about it while you are shooting. Unfortunately you are only storing up problems for the edit and it will then need correcting. A bit more time on the shoot adjusting levels will pay dividends at the edit stage.

- *Poor composition and framing* make it difficult to edit. Shots that are badly composed can look awful when edited together. For instance, on a head and shoulders shot of someone looking left to right in the frame a bad frame would be when there is not enough looking room on the right-hand side of this frame. So the nose and eyes look tight to the edge of frame and behind the head there is too much room.

If you have problems with this get some training to help refresh the basics of camera work and practice. An old method of describing good framing was "the rule of thirds," whereby a section of the screen that was a third of the way in from the left-hand side and a third of the way down from the top of the screen proves a point that is esthetically pleasing to place an item or object. This also applies to the other points around a frame that coincide with being a third in and a third down or up.

See Figures 8.1 and 8.2 for more information.

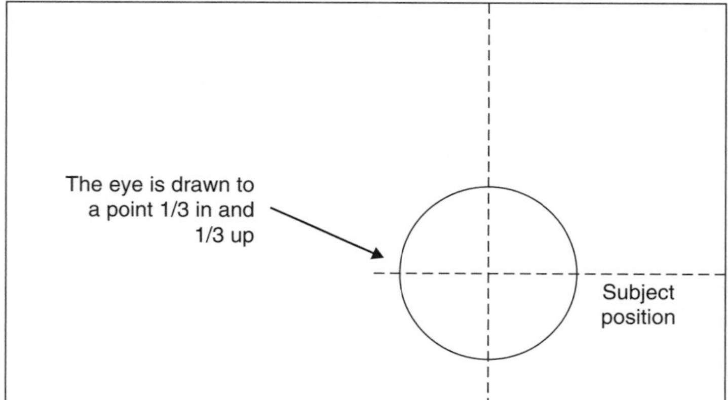

FIG 8.1 The rule of thirds as seen in the format of a video camera. A subject placed in or near the meeting of the dotted lines draws the viewers eye to it.

- *Eyelines for interviews* can be awful. It's not unusual to see the whole ear and sometimes the back of the ear of someone's head instead of two eyes.
- *Not holding a shot for long enough.* Not keeping the camera steady so every shot wobbles and makes editing hard, and the sequence looks dreadful. See above points in this chapter in the section "Single Camera Techniques for Making the Edit Go Smoothly."

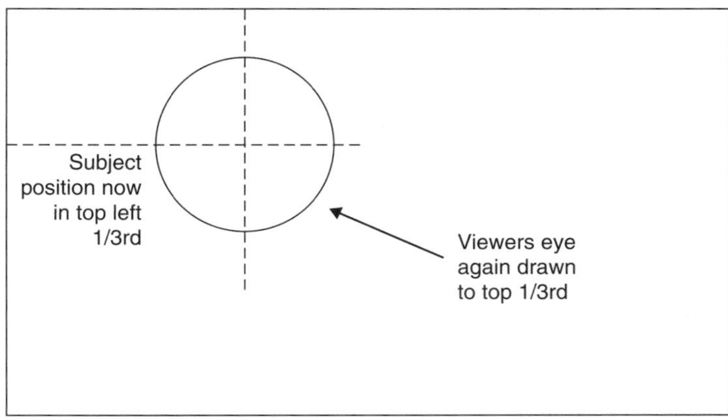

FIG 8.2
The same theory applies to any other part of the frame where the thirds meet.

- *Not enough use of the tripod* – unsteady shots. A tripod makes you concentrate on the filming and forget about moving the camera around. If the building you are shooting has interesting details visible then shoot a few very tight shots of this for good measure.
- *Hoovering or hosepiping*…where the cameraman shoots everything in sight by simply moving the camera up and down his subject but doesn't cut tape between shots and doesn't hold a shot still enough to be useful in the edit. The only solution to this is to think of how the final cut will look while you are filming. If you can't see where a clean edit can be made it is probably not possible. Hence stop recording before changing your shots.
- *Not shooting a "sequence"* in the camera. Where the cameraman shoots random shots that don't tie together, making a flowing edit impossible. The opposite of the above is where a good cameraman shoots a series of shots that do tie in and can tell the story in pictures.
- *Discontinuous time-code*. Where the cameraman has stopped and looked back at his shots but not lined the tape up at the end of the last shot. When digitizing into AVID it stops as it does not like importing over time-code breaks. Guaranteed to raise expletives in the edit suite.
- The above also makes EDLs (edit decision lists) almost unworkable.

I told you that editors were straightforward people didn't I…They want it right every time from us…

CHAPTER 9

Location Lights

Not that long ago the choice for location lighting kits was extremely limited. Many location cameramen ended up using a fairly standard kit of four redheads, which were 650 W open-faced lights with no front lens but only a movable rear parabolic reflector and so called because the light casing was a red color. These were normally accompanied by 2 kW lamps nicknamed 'blondes' due to the distinctive yellow color of their casings. Again they were open faced with no lens and a rear moveable reflector. These lamp heads were not lightweight, small, and/or subtle but every cameraman and unit manager knew what they were and what the lights could do, and they stayed as an industry standard for a long time. Luckily things have moved on; lights have become technically better, lighter, and less cumbersome to cart around.

Here is a quick look at what's around and why it's useful to us in everyday location filming. If you are new to shooting or come from a journalistic background, perhaps you shoot on SONY PD 170's or SONY HVR-Z1e's or you are an editor or soundman/woman – this chapter will help to make sense of which video lights are available. I have not tried to include every manufacturers lights but only those that are used frequently by myself and by my colleagues, or lights that solve particular filming problems effectively. So my apologies if your favorite lamps are not mentioned. And if you don't know a Dedo from a pup or a Rifa from a Diva or a key from a fill then look at the glossary of lighting terms at the end of this chapter…Don't you just love industry jargon…

My set of lights has been with me for years, I think of them in the same way I do my motorbikes – they serve the purpose well and often surprise me by how good they are.

Two questions that I get asked time and again are "How do you know what lights to use for different jobs?" and "Which lights are best for my next job?" So if you are a novice or either of these questions has ever passed your lips or been on your mind at times, then we'll look at location lights and then in the next chapters how to choose the lamps you need and tips for setups and rigs. If you are experienced with lights then skip to the following chapters, but if you need some fundamental information about location lamps or a refresher then read from here (Figures 9.1 and 9.2).

SMALLER LIGHTS – 120 TO 300 W

These are ideal sized lights for carrying around on location and coping with many types of shoots. Video cameras these days are much faster, they need less light to give a constant exposure than older cameras, and consequently you can use less light on your scenes and subjects and still get good results. This group of lights would be good for filming indoor interviews, small groups, pack shots, some exterior usage, and other everyday shoots. Many have lenses, dimmers, and barn doors with spot and flood controls, so you can be quite subtle and throw nice shadows on backgrounds with a bit of imagination. Outside in the daylight they have a limited use as they use tungsten bulbs and need a half or full blue filter or a diachronic filter to convert to daylight, which will reduce their light output on the subject.

But don't write them off too soon for exteriors because when the daylight fades and you still need to shoot, then a larger powered light can be too strong and may well overlight your subject so the lamps in this range can be more useful and allow you to balance out the background with the foreground subject. You'll have gathered by now that I am not a lover of overlighting and small f-stops with dingy, dark backgrounds…That is not what I call good lighting.

Arri 150 W junior…

- Dimmer in line available.
- Fresnel lens, barn doors.
- Sturdy-build quality in corrosion resistant aluminum, like most Arri's, will take any amount of knocks, light to carry at 1.6 kg (3.53 lb) plus stand. Arri is a trusted brand with spares and service available in many countries around the world (Figures 9.1 and 9.4).

Arri 300 W junior…

- Fresnel lens, barn doors.
- Again sturdily built a bit heavier at 2.9 kg (6.39 lb) plus stand, so it's starting to be a bit more arduous to carry around for a one-man band but a good, useful light nevertheless (Figures 9.2 and 9.4).

FIG 9.1
"Two industry standard location lights, Dedo and Arri 150W, tried and tested by cameramen the world over and strong enough to take the knocks of life on the road. My everyday lights are Dedo's."

FIG 9.2
"Next size up would be 300 W lights, here are an Arri and Sachter reporter. Still light enough to get in a kit bag and be practical for one-man band shooting."

Sachtler 300 W reporter lamp. . .

- No Fresnel lens on this lamp but it has a large output of light for a 300 and can handle outside work during the day with a blue gel on if your subject is not too far away from the lamp head.
- Lightweight at only 0.65 kg (3 lb) plus stand and easily strapped to a rucksack, in fact, you can just about get two of them packed in a kit bag.
- Spot and flood adjustment is limited and altered by use of a small lever. Not as well made, and not as refined as the others but has its merits because it's easy to lug around (Figure 9.2).

Dedo Classic DLH4. . .120/150 W

- Clever little lamp with twin aspherical lens system, which gives a high quality of light for your subjects. Unlike a Fresnel lens, this two lens setup doesn't give you a slightly darker middle ring at the center of the beam and also has clean edges to the outside of the beam throughout the whole range from spot to full flood.
- Weighs in at 558 g (1.2 lb) and only 171 mm in length. A kit of three Dedo's fits into a small carry bag along with stands, leads, gels, etc.

- Barn doors with spot and flood adjuster.
- Dimmer as standard with barn doors and lots of accessories.
- Lightweight, easy to carry. Superb for pack shots as it's so controllable and loved by cameramen over the world (Figures 9.1 and 9.5).

Giles Wooltorton, one of the team leaders at BBC Westminster, uses one Dedo and one Sachtler 300 W for most of his shooting days (Figure 9.1). He says the Sachtler works well as a fill light for live hits outside number 10 Downing Street and other exterior locations; even with a full blue on it, there is enough power for most situations. Plus it can be carried on the back of his kit rucksack.

LIGHTS FROM 200 TO 400 W

Dedo DLH200D 200 W

- Daylight-based light using twin aspheric lenses.
- High light output on end subject.
- Dimmer with mechanism to keep color temperature the same over half the power range.
- Wide focussing range.
- Weighs 1.3 kg (2.8 lb) and is only 1.74 mm in length.
- A second version of this lamp is intended for soft lighting. In Figure 9.6 you can see the bulb used to power the soft box.

FIG 9.3
"Dedo's started as 120 W tungsten lights but they have added these new series 200s and there are also 400 versions."

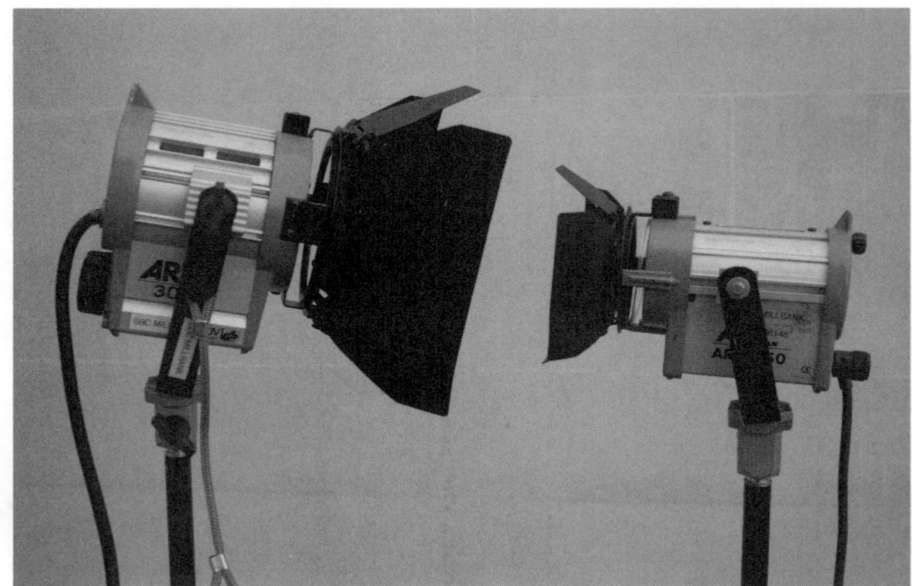

FIG 9.4
"The Arri 150W stares down his big brother 300W and hopes he'll get away with it..."

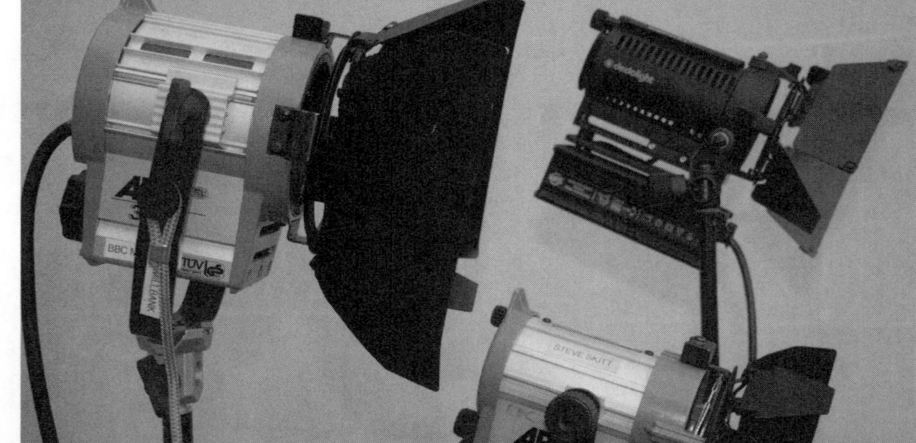

FIG 9.5
Sachtler 300 + Dedo classic along with a 150 Arri. Don't be afraid to mix your lamps if it is useful on certain shoots for you.

Dedo DLH 400 and 650

- 400 W daylight version 4.4 kg (9.7 lb) + 650 W halogen/tungsten lamp [3.4 kg (7.5 lb)] heads with double lens and all other Dedo innovations (Figure 9.7).

FIG 9.6
"Dedo's 200 range includes normal lighting heads plus soft light bulbs that fit straight into a soft box. Easy to transport and to use."

600 W TO 1 KW LAMPS

Getting bigger here, so carrying can be an issue but if you need that extra power then there is not much choice other than a larger lamp. A modern 1 kW lamp provides a lot of lighting power and if your job needs it then don't be put off getting these larger lamps.

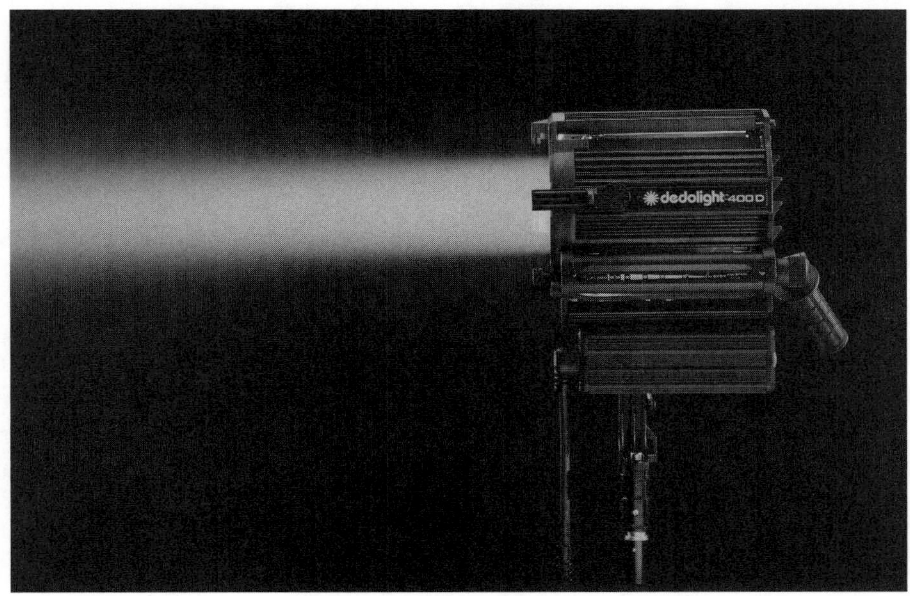

FIG 9.7
"Dedo 400 W light balanced for daylight shooting, so no need for blue correction gels to be used."

Arri 650 W lamp

- Big brother of the 300 W lamp. Same features as before, no dimmer, but will handle outside work with gels, and trace on better than the smaller lights.
- As with all Arris, it's strong and will last if looked after. At 3.6 kg (7.94 lb) plus stand, it's too big to tuck in a rucksack though.

- Six camera crews at BBC Westminster use an Arri 650 lamp on a daily basis and in all weather conditions and the final conclusion is that it's nearly indestructible (Figure 9.8).

FIG 9.8
"Arri's 650 W light is about the largest you would want to carry for any distance. It's tungsten based, 3200 K so you would need to put a blue correction gel on it to shoot outside. These are strong, rugged lights that will last a lifetime."

Arri 1 K junior

- Bigger brother of the 650 light with all the Arri attributes.
- It uses a short focal length lens that gives a wider beam of light and a higher light output. The downside as ever is the weight and the Arri 1000 W is 6 kg (13.45 lb) plus the stand.

If you still want more fire power, then Arris go up with 2 Ks and 5 Ks in their tungsten range but just expect your arms to grow longer as you cart them around.

ARRI HMI RANGE

Two hands are needed for these lights as you have the lamp plus the additional ballast box to carry, so they don't win many points for one-man band crews, unless they bring a friend along. But if you are planning on shooting outside for the whole day an HMI (Hydrargyrum Medium Arc-iodide) which is balanced for daylight will make life much easier for you once it's rigged, and also give you consistent lighting from dawn to dusk.

Starting with the Arrisun 200W that is an HMI weighing in at 3.2kg (7.05lb). If you need to see the light output of all Arri lamps then go to www.arri.com where there is a calculator that will tell you what this is with different Fresnel lenses attached to the lights.

Then the Arrisun 575 weighs in at 6.3kg (13.89lb). And the Arrisun 1200 is 15kg (33.07lb).

SOFT LIGHTS FOR LOCATION WORK

If you work as a one-man band doing camera, lights, and audio as well, then carrying a separate soft light on top of your normal camera kit may be out of the question. But you can now get soft boxes to fit over the head of your existing lights that are lightweight and fold down into small units. Or if you do have enough arms and space to carry another light, then a good choice would be one of these foldable units, or perhaps a small Kino-flow tubed soft light that produces good results.

See the chapter on lighting tips and techniques for more information about soft lights on location and the different makes available.

LIGHTING GLOSSARY

Dedo light 150W location light, invented by a film cameraman called Dedo, that has twin lenses instead of a Fresnel.

Arri Short for Arnold and Richter, who make lights, film cameras, etc.

Pup A 1kW lamp.

Basher Camera top light.

Key light The main light source in a scene. Provides the modeling for the subject and normally the most powerful of all other lights used in the scene.

Fill light Second in ranking to the key light in a scene. Positioned away from the key and nearer the camera it "fills in" the shadows on the subject from the key. Normally used at around half the power of the key light.

Backlight Comes directly from behind the subject, giving a "rim" of light to the hair and the head. Great effect to bring the subject away from the background but not the best idea in the world for using on people who are going thin on top or are completely bald. They won't thank you for it.

3/4 Backlight Comes from behind the subject again but is placed slightly to one side or the other of the subject. The light will be seen more on the side of the head, face, or top part of the body of your subject.

Kicker Like the 3/4 backlight the kicker comes from the side, farther, round to the front than the 3/4 light and gives a fuller "rim" light to the subject's face or side.

Top light Comes from directly overhead.

Soft light Any form of lighting that is not direct/hard and with a diffused source. You can put a trace, scrim, or other diffusion filter over a direct light to soften it. Well-known soft lights from manufacturers include…

Kino-flows Tubed soft light in many sizes and rugged enough for location work.

Diva light A version of the Kino-flow above.

Rifa light Lowell lights' version of a soft light/box.

Chimera Another well-known soft light/box.

Red head 650 W open-faced light.

Blonde 2 kW open-faced light.

Flags Different sized black boards used to cut out parts of the light beam and control the light/shadows.

French flag Small flag with bendy arm and clip to fasten onto many surfaces and bend round into the beam of light.

Gobo Board with shapes cut into it in order to cast patterns onto backgrounds.

Ulcer board Gobo with teardrop shapes in it.

HMI Daylight color temperature light using a separate ballast.

PAG light Well-known camera top light, powered from the camera battery, made by PAG, who also makes battery systems for video cameras.

Magic arm Useful, strong, bendy, and lockable arm to hold small lights or flags on stands or sets.

Black wrap Back tinfoil that can be shaped to cut out light and used many times over.

CTO (Color temperature orange gel), put over a daylight-based light to convert it to tungsten (3200 K).

CTB (Color temperature blue gel), put over a tungsten-based light to convert it to daylight (5600 K).

Trace/Scrim Diffusion material to make hard lights softer.

ND Neutral density filter to cut down light without altering the color temperature. Comes in 0.3, 0.6 or 0.9 grades with 0.9 being the darkest and therefore cutting out most light.

CHAPTER 10

Choosing Video Lights and Specialist Light

A few simple rules apply to every type of video and film light choice you have to make whether buying or hiring.

Lamps with lenses give a more even spread of light on your subject, and good-quality lenses give good-quality light with clean edges to the beam of light. This results in more controlled lighting for your subject.

- Look for a smooth, even adjustment of the light beam using the "spot" and "flood" adjuster knob on the lamp head (Figure 10.1). Avoid coarse, notchy adjusters as these get tiring to use over time.
- Go for a waterproof lamp; many manufacturers have had their lamps tested for this, but don't ever be tempted to use it in a heavy rainstorm.
- Make sure it's easy and quick to change bulbs on the lamps that you choose; you don't want to be fiddling around with multiple components and small screws just to change them when you are out shooting and time is against you.
- Also check that the locking wing-nuts at each stage of the lamp which allow you to adjust the height of the lamp stand are easy to operate and firmly clamp shut when done up.
- Some lamps can now use both tungsten bulbs (3200 K) and daylight bulbs (5600 K); you simply change the bulb. Good if you do as much exterior work as you do interior stuff.
- You can also buy a daylight adapter for your camera top light. PAG offers one of these, so changing from tungsten bulbs to daylight bulbs is a simple operation and both take power from the camera. The plus point is

FIG 10.1
Spot and flood adjuster. The spot and flood adjuster on this Arri lamp is placed on the rear of the lamp housing. For most normal filming you use it on the flood position where you get a wide, even spread of light.

that unlike using a blue gel over your top light, which will cut down the final light output, the daylight adapter gives more power for your subject, like a mini HMI.

- Check out the prices of spare parts before you buy a complete set of lamps and make sure there is a local distributor in your area for any servicing needs.
- Remember to ask if the manufacturer is bringing out a new lighting set in the near future to replace the ones you are being shown before you make the final decision.
- Check that the lamps meet local health and safety regulations in your country and have them PAT (portable appliance test) safety tested each year by the service agents and retain a certificate saying this has been done.

When you are choosing lights for upcoming location jobs but not entirely sure of which one to use, it can be helpful to break down the requirements of the shoot into sections and compile a bit more information about the day's work.

Choice of location lighting can be answered by thinking about different topics in two groups:

Group 1 – Practical concerns for buying lamps:

1. How many lights will I need to take with me on regular filming jobs and how many can be safely carried?

2. What is the maximum size light and minimum size light I need?
3. Choosing which wattage light you need
4. Do I need any specialist lights?
5. What lighting accessories do I need?

Group 2 – Shoot by shoot usage concerns:

6. How bright is the existing location and scene before putting up video and film lamps?
7. Will I need photographic reflectors and/or HMI lights for the exterior shots.
8. How large an area has to be lit and/or how many people need to be lit? Exterior or interior?
9. How many cameras are being used?
10. Direct lights or soft lights?
11. Can the lights be set up safely and run throughout the day without causing any danger to anyone working or moving through the nearby area and do I have an assistant to help me?
12. Is there any power in the location I can use?

HOW MANY LIGHTS WILL I NEED TO TAKE WITH ME ON REGULAR FILMING JOBS?

In the first group your lighting requirements will probably be dictated by the type of work you film day by day. So if you are a one-man band and you rush around shooting quick interviews with very little time to set up and shoot, then you are limited to one or two lights that can be packed in a small case and rigged quickly. Go for good-quality lights that are lightweight and durable. Don't forget to use a good-quality top light for your camera as this can get you out of many shooting problems. And a small reflector will always be useful as well.

However, if you do more "features"-style shooting and work as a two-man crew then you could use four lights with perhaps a nice soft light as well and a small set of flags, colored gels, and reflectors. A good-quality soft top light can be a useful extra as well (Figures 10.2–10.4).

WHAT IS THE MAXIMUM SIZE LIGHT AND MINIMUM SIZE LIGHT I NEED?

Large film and video lights provide a good spread of light to work in and anything over 1 kW with a Fresnel lens will be a useful tool, especially for bouncing

FIG 10.2
Camera top lights have come a long way from being heavy, harsh lighting units. This lamp made by Photon Beard, called a hyper-light, is only 10W and gives out a very soft light to work with. And for only 10W it provides a surprising amount of light. Its color temperature is 4000K so you can use it for both inside and outside shooting with a 1/2 blue or CTO gel if needed.

FIG 10.3
Here is the shot of the subject lit by the hyper-light above. It works as a good fill light when you use a standard key light or on its own. As you can see here the result is a pleasing soft effect.

light off reflectors or shining through soft boxes. I suppose the ultimate answer to the question is that we really need everything from an 18K HMI lamp through to a 20W tungsten camera top light, but think of the size of the car you'll need for that lot…So back to reality…

FIG 10.4
When I shoot features for GMTV in the U.K. I regularly use this larger soft light which runs on daylight tubes. We work as a two-man crew. Ian Birch is the sound recordist and runs the outfit, so rigging and carrying this larger soft light is not a problem. But a one-man band would have a problem unless someone else was there to help out.

If you are shooting high end interviews or trying to balance a brightly lit room or exterior a few larger-powered lights will be far more useful than choosing many more smaller lights. Don't forget when you are on location it's more effective to cut the light output down on a bigger lamp by using ND gel (Neutral density filter) over the front of it than to use more smaller lights very close to your subject. The larger lamps can be rigged away from the subject and camera helping to maximize the working area for the crew. But larger lamps are heavier and you may well need an assistant to help you rig and control them. So don't be tempted to go too large if it's not needed.

TIP
If you are using lights for a long period of shooting and they are right at the top of their lighting stands, then always stabilize the bottom of the stand with sandbags or weighted kit bags placed over the bottom of the stands. This is also good in windy conditions outdoors.

On the other end of the scale don't go for the smallest wattage lamp when you could use a slightly larger one with an in-line dimmer. This effectively gives you two lamps in one and will be useful in far more circumstances than a very small one would be. For example a 300 W lamp with a dimmer will be more useful in different locations than a 150 W lamp without a dimmer.

FIG 10.5
Which wattage light is best? At a constant exposure of f5.6, the 650 W light is 2.4 m further away from the subject than the 150 W. If you had used the 650 W light in a small room you would undoubtedly be over-lighting your subject unless you used ND filter on the light plus you have the added problem of carrying the heavier lamp with you to and from the location. The extra power of the 650 W is wasted in this situation. But if the subject was sitting in front of a window then the extra power of the 650 W would allow you to expose for the window whilst balancing the light on the subject as you would have to work with a smaller f-stop.

CHOOSING WHICH WATTAGE LIGHT YOU NEED

To help you choose the correct wattage lamp to take on jobs have a look at Figures 10.5 and 10.6, which show the difference of light produced by three standard video lamps; Arri 150, 300, and 650 W. Figure 10.5 shows us that at a decent working exposure of f5.6 (measured by my Ikegami DVCAM with a Canon lens), a subject lit by the 150 W lamp will be 1.1 m from the subject. To achieve the same exposure with the 300 W the distance is 2.0 m and for the 650 W the distance will be 3.5 m. All lights are direct and at full flood position.

Figure 10.6 shows all three lamps positioned 2.0 m away from the subject and the change in brightness that they give due to the power difference. This is shown as a working exposure in f-stops and you can see that there is a difference of 2.5 f-stops between the 650 and 150 W. Again all lights are at full flood and direct. So if you are planning to have a wide aperture and use this to help throw the background out of focus the smaller light would be easier to work with and more practical to carry around. Again the bigger light is wasted for this job because you would have to use an ND filter to reduce the output and get the wider f-stop that the 150 W light would give you.

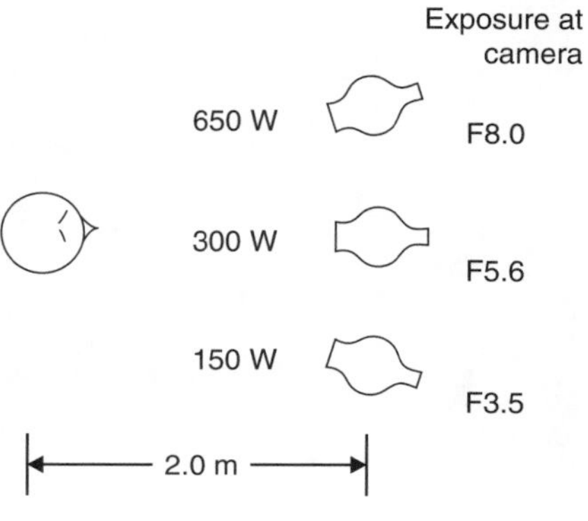

FIG 10.6
Unless you need to work with a smaller aperture or can only position the light a good distance from your subject then the 650's power is wasted as even the little 150 W light will give you a good working f-stop of f3.5.

SPECIALIST LIGHTS

Some specialist lights give great results in tricky location situations and are well worth thinking about. Around the lens lights or ring lights have normally been the weapon of choice for glossy pop promos when they want to get a shadowless light falling on the subject. Now these lights are available for most video cameras, even for the smaller prosumer types (Figure 10.7).

If you are shooting a documentary and are moving from one scene to another quickly and without much time to rig lights, this ring light can keep a constant illumination on your subjects as they move from one area to the next. This will give you a steady light for the whole take and a constant color temperature on your subjects. Look at the still shown in Figure 10.8, with a lens-lite shooting on

FIG 10.7
Their ring light is fitted on to a SONY Z1. Apart from making pop stars look good they also fulfill other useful purposes as well.

FIG 10.8
Fantastic solution to a tricky problem and you can use them on many cameras now from 35 mm film down to Z1's.

a dog sled team – how cool is that?…You can just imagine how difficult it would be to get a constant light and exposure in these conditions without this type of lamp. I assume another plus point was the small amount of power needed to use this light, which would have been useful on this type of shoot. But any

shoot where you are following someone around in varying lighting conditions would benefit from this lamp.

To highlight how clever this light can be in certain circumstances, I know of a production company that only does "red-carpet" interviews of movie stars on film premieres. This company found that it was more likely to get the big stars coming up to its camera on premiere nights if it had a lens-lite on it. The stars knew that the light from this little lamp is softer and more flattering than a normal camera top light…Another clever way around a problem…and a few more bucks made as well…

Another useful light is the Kino-flow barfly, which is a small soft tube lamp of 100 or 200 W. It is small enough to be tucked into small, hard to get to areas or even built into sets. Or it can also be held by hand. Good for us in small tricky sets or offices (Figure 10.9).

FIG 10.9
The lightweight Kino-flow barfly lamp, useful for location shooting in tight places.

Another type of light that is becoming more and more popular and has great advantages is an LED camera top light (Figure 10.10). This has benefits over the older fashioned PAG top light with conventional bulbs.

Powered from the camera's 12 V socket these lights consume less power than normal bulbs. Some like this Gekko k-lite also have a dimmer in line and a diffusion filter, which can swing over the lamp as well. You can also get extension

FIG 10.10
LED camera light….

arms that swing the lamp off the camera and allow to model the light falling on the subject better. They are also quite light in weight.

Another useful lighting development are the litepad by Rosco. I came across these at a tech show recently and couldn't help thinking how useful they would be for location shooting. They come in six different sizes from 76 mm × 76 mm

up to 304 mm × 304 mm. At 7.6 mm thick the litepad is a slim profile LED light giving a soft light source and a daylight-based color temperature. From a location cameraman's point of view they have some good benefits, such as being very lightweight, running off mains and batteries, and because they are so thin you could pack two or three in a rucksack working with your own lamps or on their own. They would be good fill lights in vehicles and helpful in very small locations, they don't emit as much heat as other video lights and where normal lamps would take up too much room (Figures 10.11 and 10.12).

FIG 10.11
The future of video lighting? Rosco's Litepads, thin, light LED slabs only 7.6 mm thick. You could carry three of these tucked inside your rucksack and they would only be as thick as a paperback book.

WHAT LIGHTING ACCESSORIES DO I NEED?

Again if you are a small crew or a one-man band keep it small and light. Here is my kit for the work I do for BBC as a one-man band (Figure 10.13). All the essentials are here but no more as I do up to 12 interviews per day all in different locations. I bring an extra kit only when I need it…Small and light is lovely…

However, you will need an RCD (Residual current device), correcting gels, 1/2 blues, etc., trace, and ND plus clips and mains cable. For larger lights and bigger shoots just bring more of these and any flags and gobos that could be used.

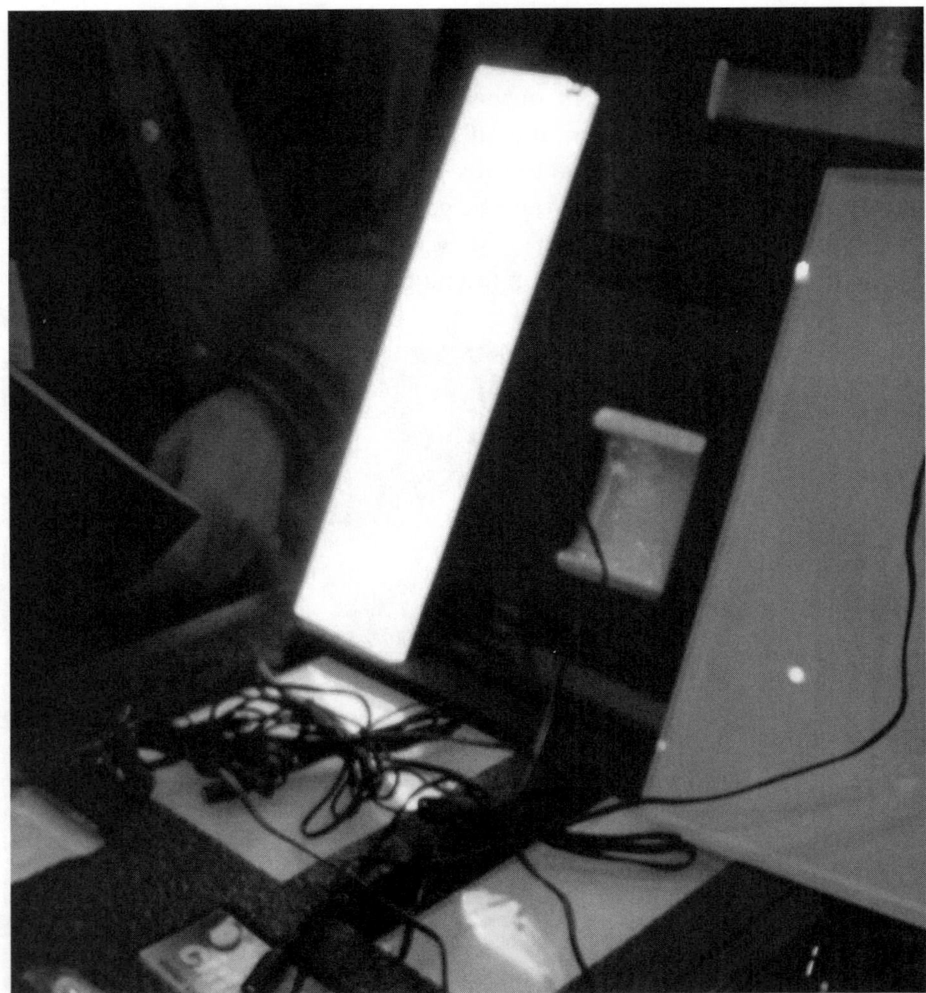

FIG 10.12
Litepad in box. Rosco's litepads, only 7.6 mm thick. You could carry three of these tucked inside you rucksack and they would only be as thick as a paperback book.

HOW BRIGHT IS THE EXISTING LOCATION AND SCENE BEFORE PUTTING UP VIDEO AND FILM LAMPS?

In group 2 this first question can only be answered if you know more about the proposed shooting locations, so if you are rushing around filming on a tight schedule and with limited information the chances are you won't be able

FIG 10.13
Typical one man band shooting kit, all the essentials to provide good quality audio and video are here and pack away into a rucksack. The lighting filters are a sheet of ½ blue gel, sheet of 0.3 ND Filter, sheet of diffusion filter and four clips. Other gels are kept in my locker ready to be added as needed.

to answer this as it's out of your control. But your producer/director or unit manager should have given you a brief rundown of the day's requirements anyway along with an idea of lighting conditions at the location. If you do have this information you can decide whether to use and work with the ambient light, and supplement this with your lamps or use your video and film lamps to light everything from scratch. As I'm sure you are aware, the second option will be much more complex and time consuming, especially if it's a large area, as you'll have to order in lamps as needed. However, 90% of the time the real-world answer will be to use the existing light and supplement it with the lights you have in order to create the required effect on screen.

But if you are lacking info the safest way of approaching the day's work is to use your normal location lighting kit with 1–4 lightweight lamps, stands, color correction gels, diffusion material, ND gels, clips, mains leads, and RCD units. Only take the minimum kit needed if you are constantly moving locations and make sure other crew members help with the carrying.

TIP
If you are working with a production team let them know before the shoot that you intend taking your normal lighting kit and what is included in that kit. By opening the subject before the shoot happens your colleagues can let you know if there are any special lighting circumstances that will affect the shoot and if you can shoot without lights in that location.

If you know in advance that you have to light people outside on a sunny day then the challenge will be to balance out the sun with a light that can fill in the shadows on people's faces and avoid hard contrasty light and shadows from the sun.

There are two ways around this.

REFLECTORS

The simplest option is to carry a foldable photographic or lighting reflector, made by Lastolight and other companies, with one white side and the other silver or gold. These can be held by other crew members or, if the day is not too windy, can be mounted on a light stand and positioned as needed.

Don't fall into the trap of trying to get the reflected light falling on the subject to be exactly the same level as the sunny side of the person's face, especially with the silver/gold sides of the reflector. You'll simply make it very uncomfortable for the guest by pushing the reflector close to him or her and it will also look terrible as the light from the colored side of a reflector, when held close to the subject, is very hard and bright. It will show every wrinke. Use the reflector subtly to gently fill in the darker side of the person and it will give good results (Figure 10.14). Always try the white side first as it produces a softer light quality on the face than the silver/gold, which can be too harsh.

FIG 10.14
Reflector and sun on the guest's face.
"Use the reflector as if it were a fill-in light and try to even out the light from the opposite angle of the sun falling on the guest's face. The result should be a balanced light falling on the guest's face."

HMI LIGHTS

The other choice will need a power supply and if you have this you can use a daylight-based HMI light or use a tungsten light with a blue gel. My choice for HMIs would be to use Arri's as they are tried and tested. HMIs come in many sizes, from monster 12/18K switchables but a good all round size for day by day working is the Arrisun 2 as seen in Figure 10.15.

HMIs up to about 1200W can be rigged by one person but after that you really need an assistant as they become physically difficult to control on your own due to size and weight. Many HMIs now have dimmers included. Arris do, which make them more useful throughout a long day as you can balance the light's output to match the sun's level.

And tungsten lights go from 5000W down to camera top lights of 50 or 20W. Again many have dimmers in line. This second route of using lamps outside will obviously be more time consuming, but if you need to control the light over a long period of shooting this is the best method. If the shoot has the budget and it's important to get good, consistent results go for the route of having the right lamps; it's the only way to get good pictures over a long day.

(a)

(b)

FIG 10.15

(a) Arrisun 2 HMI light head. (b) And don't forget that you will have to carry the ballast box that HMI lights always need.

So if you know you are filming outside in the evening or nighttime you only need bring low-wattage lights as the existing ambient light will be less powerful than during the day. As a rule a 1K or 650W light with a blue gel would provide enough output for filming outside throughout the late afternoon and into the evening. If you need less light from it when night falls an ND gel will help lower the power. If you are working in the evening and nighttime lamps between 300 and 150W will normally suffice. Depending on your background even a 50W lamp at night can be effective as it allows the camera to work on a wider f-stop and allows you that coveted shallow depth of field.

Last note on this is that if you don't know how the day's filming is going to go regarding lighting, it's better to have a more powerful light and reduce the light by dimmers or ND filters than to have a small light and not enough power.

HOW LARGE AN AREA HAS TO BE LIT AND HOW MANY PEOPLE?

The second point is easier to decide upon. If you are filming a larger area and you have to light the foreground guests plus the background, or if people are walking and moving through the shot, you simply have to have more lamps to cover it. A single light might have a useful spread of light of about 3m when it is set to full flood and pulled back from the subject but if, for example, you are panning and following people through an area wider than this allow multiple lights, possibly one lamp per 3m width, to get an even throw over the width of your scene. Use separate lights to illuminate the background, and if you need to backlight your subject allow more lights for this purpose.

EXTERIOR OR INTERIOR

A small office could be easily lit with 2–4 tungsten lights of between 150 and 300W each. Two lamps could be the key lights for two subjects, and if they are seated and facing each other you might get the bonus of using each key as a backlight for the other person. If not, you can use the remaining lights as two backlights or as background lights with one of them used to throw an interesting shadow onto the wall.

Thus HMI lights or tungsten lights with blue gels will give more control. We discussed them in the section "HMI Lights" above.

HOW MANY CAMERAS ARE BEING USED?

If you are just lighting for one camera then all the above notes apply. But if you are using two or more cameras at the same time for shooting then allow for more lights to cover each camera. The minimum would be one more light per camera, which would act as a fill light from that camera's point of view. Add more if you need to backlight subjects filmed by separate cameras.

DIRECT LIGHTS OR SOFT LIGHTS?

Up to now we've been using direct lights, which you would find in any location lighting kit. If you need to shoot with softer light there are a few ways to solve this. The tried and tested method of putting diffusion trace or spun over the lights will give a softer source, but will also become less controllable as the light will now spill out and cover a wider area. Or bounce the lights off reflectors or white walls. But the most controllable method is to have a soft box with an egg-crate or louver on the front and put the lamp head through this. The egg-crates or louvers stop the soft light from spreading too wide and keep the majority of light on the subject.

Chimera makes good soft boxes, and others are available from different makers (Figures 10.16 and 10.17).

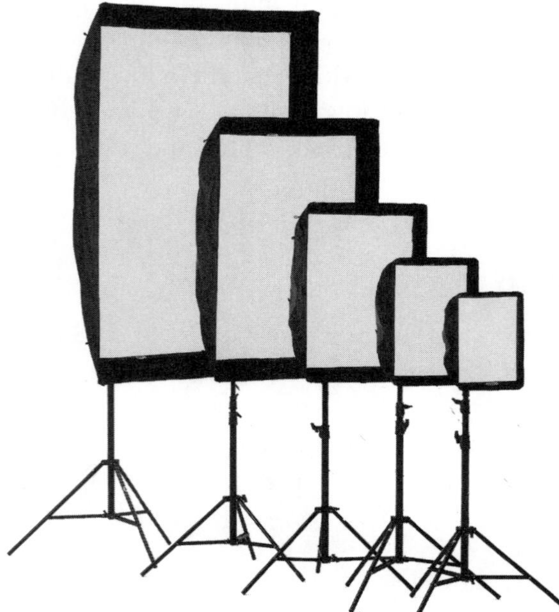

FIG 10.16
Five Chimera soft lights in action from large to small. A larger soft light source will always give a better result as the light tends to wrap around the subject.

FIG 10.17
Chimeras with egg-crate or louver.
"This Chimera is having a fabric egg-crate or louver put on it to save any spill light hitting other parts of the set. Good for location work as it will fold down into a small packet when not being used. Most other soft light manufacturers will have a system for cutting out spill light. It keeps your lighting clean and workable and stops any bounced light getting back on the subject."

They are well made, and with a 1K lamp or more will give a good usable light for your subject, very soft and very flattering. Use a soft light as a key, a direct light as a backlight, and add a smaller soft fill light with approximately half the power of the key light to get a good end result.

Many camera people have very definite views about using soft light for every setup and not using direct light at all. It's one of those filming topics that people can get really worked up about, and that's putting it mildly. Soft lighting gives great results when used correctly. But a soft light that is placed in a bad position in relation to the subject will give a poor result. When I was in my first year as a trainee cameraman I asked a long-standing film DP (director of photography in the U.S., or DP in the U.K.) if soft light was better than hard direct light. The answer was "Neither one is better than the other, the key to good lighting is placing the lamp exactly where it will do the best job." "Look at some of the old black and white films where they only used direct light but it was controlled perfectly. Use the right light in the right situation."

Let me try and explain this a bit further as you are definitely going to come across this argument in the future. In Figure 10.18 setup A has a direct light, on full flood, keying the subject to give the camera the benefit of the shadow side of the face toward the camera, and has been adjusted to get the best result on the subject's face both in how high it is, so you don't get a long nose shadow, and how far from the camera it is, so it is not too hot on one side of the face. The fill light is 1/2 as powerful as the key and comes from just to the right of the camera toward the key side. The backlight is directly behind the subject and adjusted to get a nice rim of light around the head and not give a long shadow from the ears.

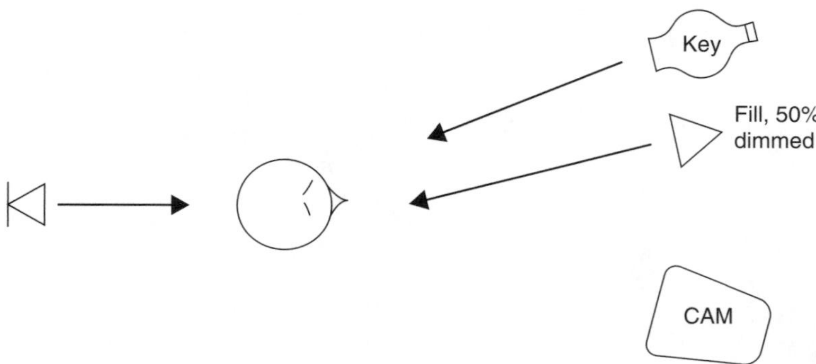

FIG 10.18
Direct lights correctly positioned to give a classic "shadow to camera look" on the subject.

Setup B has a light being bounced against a reflector to give the shadow side to camera, the key light is soft and placed similarly to setup A, and the backlight is also soft (Figure 10.19).

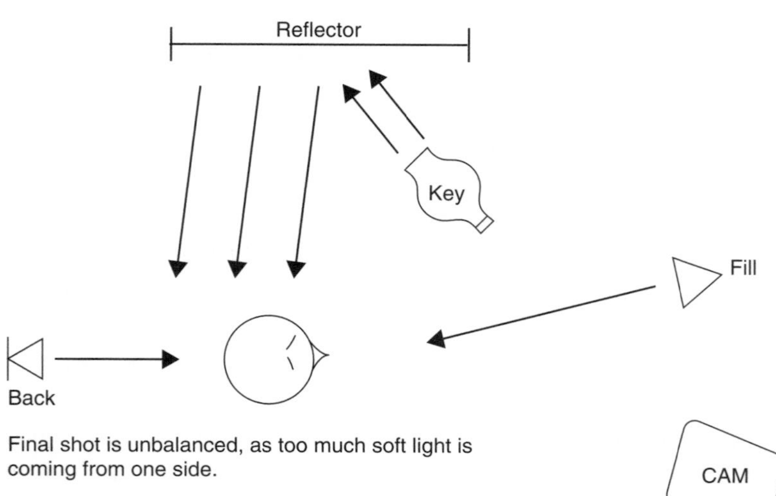

FIG 10.19
Whereas this soft light rig is going to look unbalanced with too much light coming from the reflector.

What do we see on the monitor? The first setup, which has been nicely adjusted for the subject, provides good, balanced lighting and flatters. You are unaware that the light is hard because it has been adjusted perfectly for the subject. The second setup has the key light too far to the right so the light across both sides of the face does not balance at all; one side is hotter than the other. As the fill light is also on the same side it is increasing the light on that side and aiding the imbalance of light on the face. The soft backlight is not strong enough to have much affect and too low so ear shadows are appearing.

The point I'm making here is that badly rigged soft lights will look worse than a correctly rigged direct/hard light. Soft light works well and flatters but it's not going to do it if it's badly rigged and positioned, and in some cases it's simply the wrong light to use.

It's a similar argument to an editor choosing to use mixes or soft edge wipes as transitions between shots instead of hard cuts in an edit. You've probably noticed this before but if you use a lot of mixes to get from one shot to another in a sequence your eye gets used to this type of transition and the thought of a hard cut becomes almost repulsive. But a good editor uses hard cuts perfectly, and when you see the finished clip played back it flows just as smoothly as if there were wipes, only it's faster and keeps the pace up more.

CAN THE LIGHTS BE SET UP SAFELY AND RUN THROUGHOUT THE DAY WITHOUT CAUSING ANY DANGER TO ANYONE WORKING OR MOVING THROUGH THE NEARBY AREA, AND DO I HAVE AN ASSISTANT TO HELP ME?

If you are working in busy offices or near corridors any lights you set up have to be safe and not liable to be knocked over. Use a kit bag to hang over the base of the light stand to keep it steady. Similarly any mains cables leading to them will have to be covered by rubber matting so people don't trip over them. If you have an assistant he or she can help rig the lamps and keep an eye on them while you film. If you are there all day a helper is essential.

IS THERE ANY POWER IN THE LOCATION I CAN USE?

Sounds obvious, but if you can't gain access to power there's no point in bringing the mains powered lighting kit. Always ask about power circuits before plugging your lamps in. If some circuits are dedicated to all the offices' computers it's safer to use another circuit, so in the event of your lamp having a breakdown it doesn't affect the computers. Always check that you are not overloading plugs and circuits with your lamps.

SAFETY AND LIGHTING

It's always worth considering the safest way of working when using any electrical appliances, and film and video lights are no different than other electric powered units when it comes to this. In Chapter 15 there is a lot more information that is relevant to location lighting so have a look at that chapter and see how you can make your normal working routine even safer while filming on location.

CHAPTER 11

Location Lighting Tips and Setups

In Chapter 6 we looked at an interior lighting setup than can work on location using 1–3 lamps and which you can change and adapt to suit many situations but should give you good results even on the busiest day.

In this chapter I'll describe how to use different video lights and look at some location lighting setups, both interior and exterior, that are tried and tested and provide useful, simple solutions for many professional cameramen shooting on location. They are straightforward to rig and use and again you can adapt them for the type of shooting you do and the locations that you find yourself in.

As always the rigs described here are "real-world" setups used by professional cameramen everywhere because they work regularly, are quick to rig, and can be adapted to many situations and locations. They are tried and tested.

So let's start by moving one step forward from the setup in Chapter 6 and see how we can improve the look and feel of the scenes that we shoot by using our lighting to help add extra visual elements along with a bit of imagination.

CREATING AND LIGHTING BETTER BACKGROUNDS

I always find it most frustrating when I turn up to shoot at an office, house, or similar location only to find that we have been given a small plain room or area to film in, making it hard to light properly and meaning the subject is pushed up against the background, and giving you no chance at all to separate the two elements. If the wall is just a plain, blank area, then you know the shot will be boring and uninteresting.

TIP
Put a green lighting gel over the lamp, lighting the plant, as it will enrich the green leaves of the plant and the shadows falling onto the wall from the plant will also have a nice green hue.

I'm sure that in this situation you've all got one eye open for any object or items that will break up the background such as a plant, some books, or a picture. If the plant is floor standing you can light it with a separate, direct, hard light and allow the shadows to fall onto the wall as well. This helps break up a plain background well (Figure 11.1).

FIG 11.1
Shadow of a plant on the on wall behind the guest's seat.
"It's an old trick but yes, it works and creates a much better background for your guests to be filmed against."

If you can't use a plant try putting light, shadows, patterns, and color onto the background.

We will assume that the location is not too brightly lit from outside with no direct sunlight spilling into the room, and we can then use small video lights, between 150 and 300W, which is a good range to choose from for small areas like this. That will keep the video lighting low and personal and will create a good feel and style. Lamps with dimmers are particularly good in these small areas.

Use a direct key light, not bounced light (as the bounced light will flood the whole scene because it is such a small area) and try to keep this key lamp from illuminating the back wall behind the subject by having the light a bit on the

higher side on the stand so the shadow from the subject falls onto the floor and the lower part of the wall behind. This shadow is then hidden by the subject and away from camera view. Using the barn doors (or lighting flags if you have them) you should be able to keep excess light away from the wall behind the subject (Figures 11.2 and 11.3).

TIP
Remember to white balance again if you dim the video lights because the color temperature will have changed and the lights will be running "warmer," with a lower color temp.

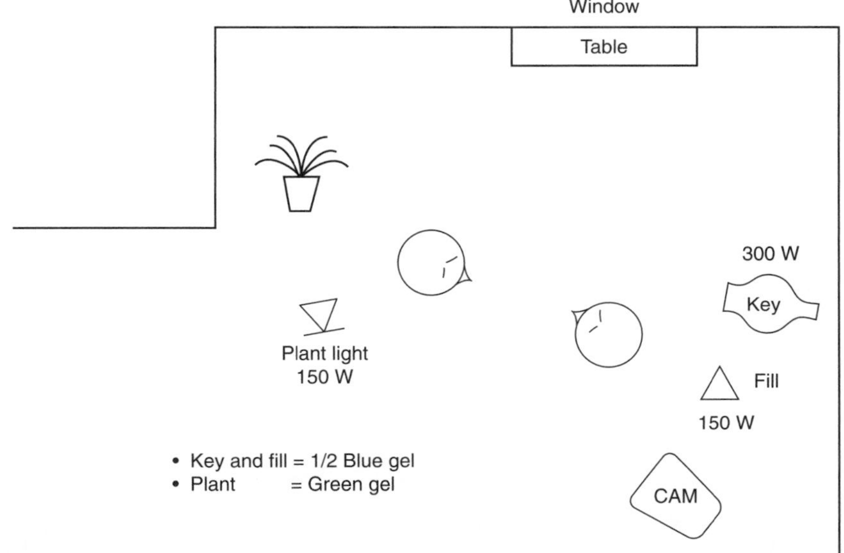

FIG 11.2
Setup of lights from above.
"Here's the location lighting as seen from above showing which lights we are using and their positions. There is no room for a backlight as the location is so small, but a shadow from the plant will help."

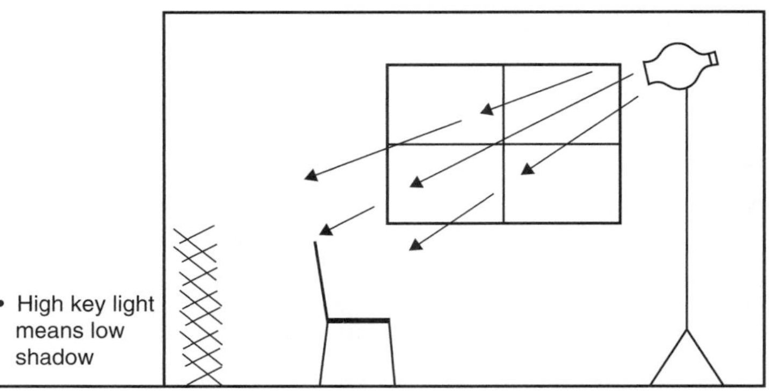

FIG 11.3
Setup of lights from floor level.
"From the floor point of view you can see the height of each lamp, and the key light throwing its shadow behind the guest and low enough not to be seen by the camera. This leaves the wall background clear to accept a pattern or shadow."

Then you can try putting some interesting shadows and color onto the wall itself from another angle. Get another light and position it behind the subject but pointing at the wall. Add some colored gel, whatever shade you feel is pleasant, and shine it on the wall, making sure it doesn't hit the subject. Now you could introduce some shadows to this color wash using lighting flags and make it more interesting to the eye. You can of course use the plant shadow from a light with a green gel on it, as we mentioned earlier, to create a good pattern on the background as well.

SHADOWS, PATTERNS AND GOBO'S

Figures 11.4–11.7 show a variety of shadows and patterns that help to break up the background and create visual interest. Again they work best when the key light is direct and not bounced as mentioned above. All these backgrounds are from a 150W Dedo light, which is less than 2m from the wall itself. I've used the Dedo image projector attached to the Dedo lamp to throw the image onto the background and then softened it slightly to give the effect of a shallow depth of field. The imager works well in cramped spaces. In these shots, it is no more than 1.5m away from the wall itself but you can still control its output and softness (Figure 11.8).

FIG 11.4
"The location is lit but no patterns have been used on the background yet."

FIG 11.5
"The first of three shadow patterns: blinds or slats that could realistically be coming from another window."

FIG 11.6
Example 2 is a simple spot effect."

What you can't see in the photographs is that all the patterned backgrounds have a blue color to them, which contrasts well with the tungsten light falling on the subject.

FIG 11.7
"All three shadows do the job of creating some background interest to a simple location and adding to production values it's your choice which one looks best."

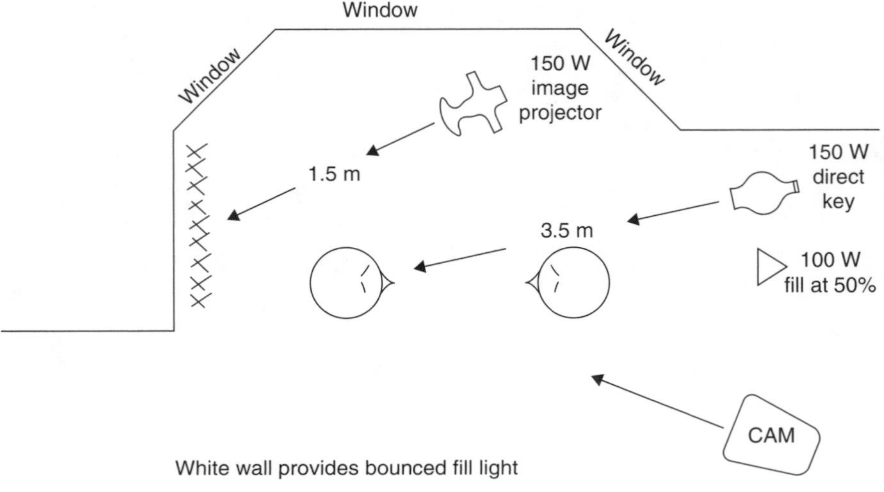

FIG 11.8
Lighting plot of above setup from above.

In film and video lighting jargon the tools we use to create patterned shadows or shapes on backgrounds are called flags, gobo's, Charlie bars, or ulcer boards, and they come in all sizes, but they are basically just plastic or wooden shapes that are supported on another lighting stand that you then put in between your lamp and the wall (Figures 11.9 and 11.11).

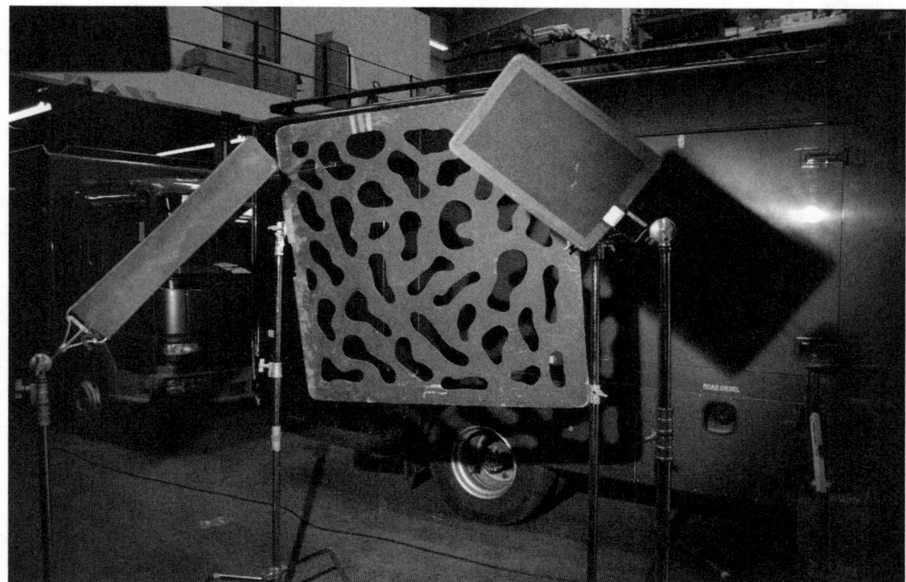

FIG 11.9
Selection of gobo's, flags, and ulcer boards. "Shadow makers... create backgrounds to die for on your next shoot."

Most lighting companies carry shadow makers for sale or hire or you can make your own. A very simple way that I've used many times before is to cut two strips of cardboard and position them as a "V" on a second lamp stand and project this shadow onto the wall (Figure 11.10).

The Dedo Image projector is very versatile and can also use shutter blades which are quite easily inserted into the front of the lamp and then you use these to make different shapes and patterns with the blades in order to project them on the walls or surfaces. Now once you've done this, you can focus the shapes or shadow onto your surface. But by keeping the projected pattern slightly out of focus you can create the all-important effect that there is less depth of field between the subject and the background than there actually is. This then gives you that satisfying shallow depth of field, albeit in an artificial way, and brings the subject away from the background. And again you can use this technique with any video camera from a palmcorder through to an HD Sony HDCAM (Figure 11.12).

FIG 11.10
Paul's flag setup. "Homemade flags from cardboard box tops, but effective nonetheless."

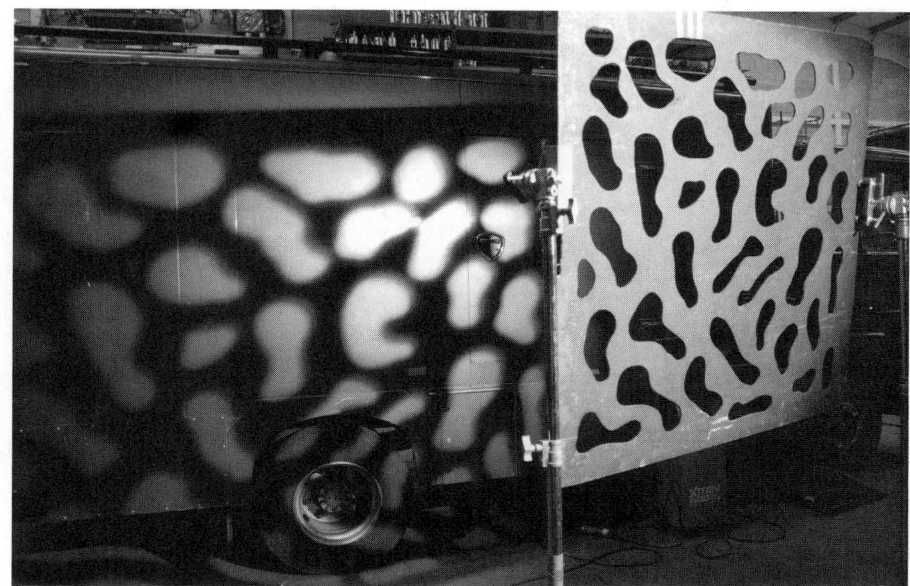

FIG 11.11
"Professional ulcer board throwing dappled patterns on the set."

FIG 11.12
Dedo with an image projector on it…
"Ideal for putting precise patterns and shadows onto backgrounds, the image projector can be used effectively in tight areas and scenes. You can also defocus the image as well. This technique can be used for any type of video or film camera."

FIG 11.13
"Purpose built set showing the effect of a background image."

If you were shooting a corporate video and you needed to get the client's name and logo on the background behind your subject, you can use the image projector to do this. You need to have the sign or image made up as a purpose built gobo that slots into the projector. This is a very handy and a cheap way to get a good professional effect.

Shadows on a background are as important as light falling on a background (Figure 11.13). Look at some of the old black and white movies and see how the lighting cameramen used shadows and background shapes to fill up parts of the frame – they were masters. Some shots contained more shadows than light but the final effect was stunning.

Take a look at Figure 11.14 of a typical domestic filming setup with and without a background effect light. It's another variation to the ones above in the small corridor, showing again that the technique can work in many locations. It looks as if the slash of light is coming from the table lamp (but it isn't). It's all comparative.

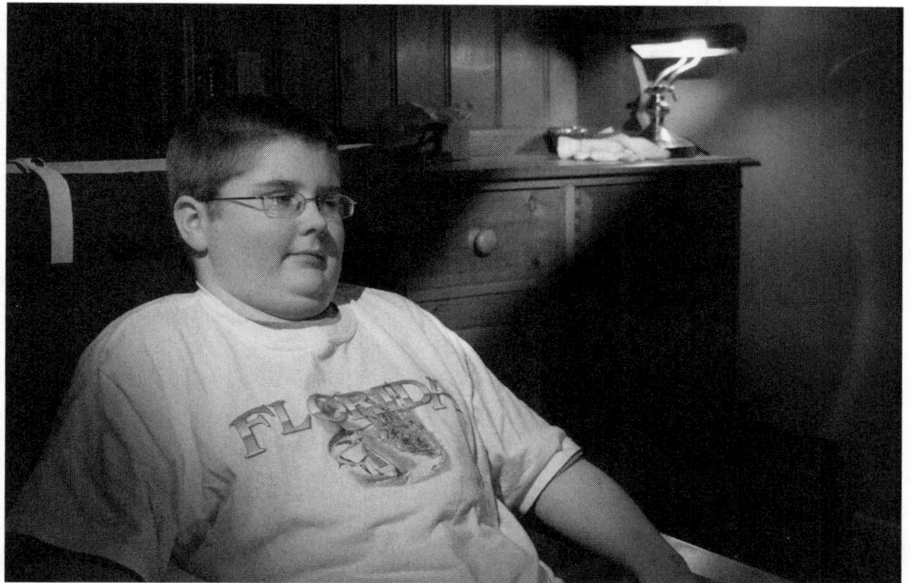

(a)

(b)

FIG 11.14
Lighting illusion? "The slash of light in the background comes from a video light. It helps give the illusion that's from the table light and again creates visual interest."

SOFT LIGHT TECHNIQUES

Up to now the lighting described has been hard light and directional with the emphasis on positioning the lamp heads in the right place. Now we'll take a look at using softer light and how to control it. But as always the most important aspect of video/film lighting is deciding where you place the lamp, and this applies for both hard light and soft light. Positioning the light/lamp is crucial. Soft light works really well on video but a badly positioned soft light will not look good.

One of the simplest and quickest ways to change hard light into soft light on location is by placing a sheet of trace or diffusion filter over the front of the lamp, which I'm sure you already know. But as soon as you do this, the light from the lamp will spread out and cover a larger area than the direct light. By doing this, it becomes harder to control and keep off the background and side areas. The same effect occurs when you "bounce" the light off a wall or reflector onto the scene. It spreads in all directions and covers the entire scene unless it is controlled.

For instance, let's look again at the shots taken in the smallish corridor and window area with the guest seating as in Figures 11.4–11.7. The lights here are direct and any spill light has been controlled by the barn doors on the lamp heads so it doesn't cover the pillars to the side of the guest and only hits a very small area of the background behind the guest, also helped by the light being high enough to push the shadow of the guest low down the wall. This keeps the lighting on the scene clean and controllable.

If we then put a trace gel over the key light, we will lose that control immediately, and although the light falling on the guest will be softer, it will also cover the whole scene randomly as in Figure 11.15.

FIG 11.15
Soft light in corridor setting.
"The diffusion filter has softened the light on our subject but also increased the spread of light to cover the entire area."

And if you are filming in a small area such as in this example the soft light will basically fall on every surface and bounce around the scene. So we lose any control over this spill of light, and the ability to keep the walls that are behind the subject but still in our shot nicely shadowed disappears.

In the real world of day-to-day filming there are two scenarios that can solve the problem above. You either have access to good, modern, soft source lamp heads, which will have a method of controlling the spill, or you use flags. But if you have an older set of lights, the chances are that you will have to use diffusion gels to place over the front of them in order to create a soft source.

In the first case your lighting kit will have optional accessories called "egg-crates," "honeycombs," "louvers," or something similar. This is an accessory that looks like a black grid of squares, which goes over the front of the lamp head and controls the spill of the soft light, allowing it to fall on your subject and not on other parts of the scene (Figure 11.16).

(a)

FIG 11.16
Soft lights with lowers prics "Controlled soft lighting from a small lamp, useful for many location cameramen."

We'll look at these later. But if you only have the use of standard film and video lights and gels, what do you do for control?

Use lighting flags similar to the ones we discussed creating better backgrounds and controlling the shadows behind a subject (Figures 11.17 and 11.18).

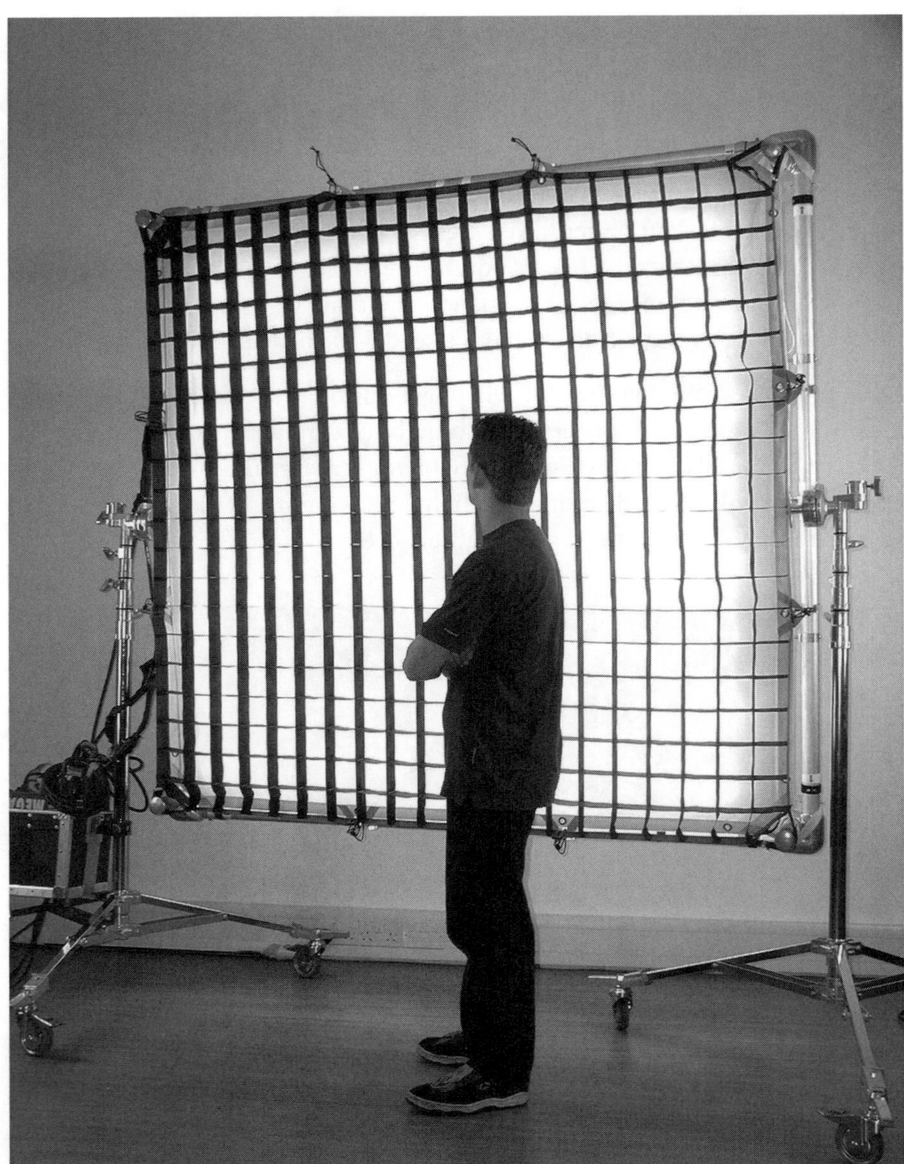

(b)

FIG 11.16
Large sets need large lights. "But the method of control is still the same, louvers or honeycombs concentrate the light onto the subject and off the background."

Place the flags on a lighting stand in front of the soft lamp head using the edge of the flag to keep the main beam on the subject but cut excess light off the surrounding area. Alter the hardness/softness of the shadow line by moving it closer or farther from the light source. Now you can allow the light to fall

FIG 11.17
Flag being used to cut out light on a wall. "Flags used to control spill from a lamp with diffusion material clamped on the barn doors. There is still some random spill light due to the diffusion material."

FIG 11.18
"If you take the diffusion material off the lamp then the shadow becomes cleaner, like this."

> **TIP**
> If the flag is a large one, remember to weigh down the lighting stand so it doesn't topple over accidentally.

neatly on your subject but you have controlled the amount and effect of the light on the background and side walls with the flag. You can use multiple flags to keep light off other areas or clamp black wrap onto the flag and create shadow areas this way.

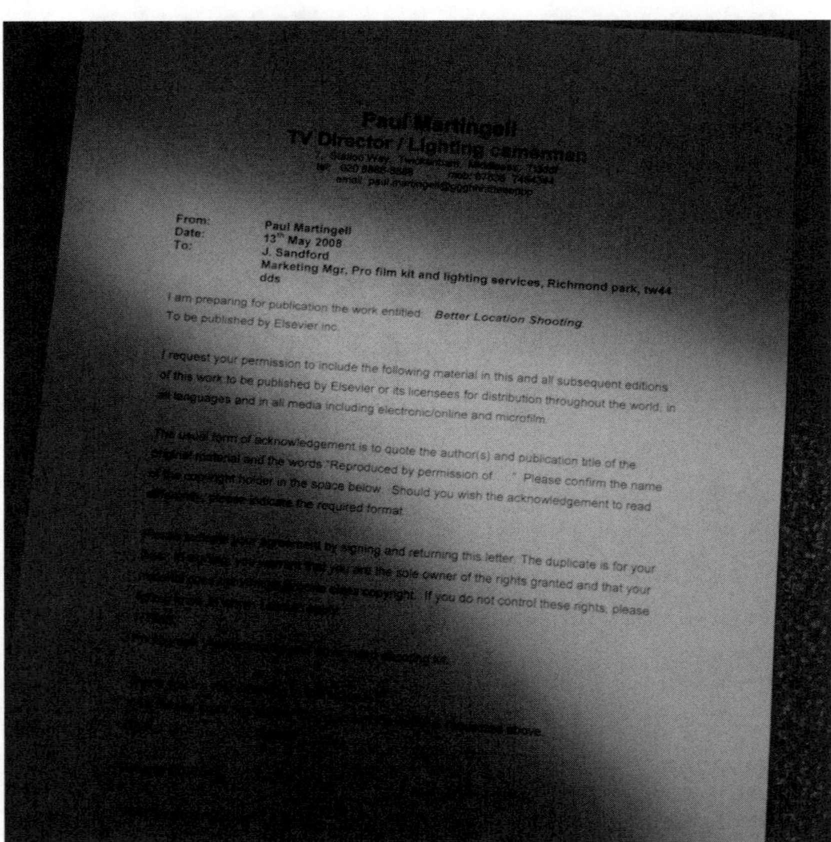

Paul Martingell
TV Director / Lighting cameraman

From: Paul Martingell
Date: 13th May 2008
To: J. Sandford
Marketing Mgr, Pro film kit and lighting services, Richmond park, tw44
dds

I am preparing for publication the work entitled *Better Location Shooting*
To be published by Elsevier inc.

I request your permission to include the following material in this and all subsequent editions of this work to be published by Elsevier or its licensees for distribution throughout the world, in all languages and in all media including electronic/online and microfilm.

The usual form of acknowledgement is to quote the author(s) and publication title of the original material and the words "Reproduced by permission of ..." Please confirm the name of the copyright holder in the space below. Should you wish the acknowledgement to read differently, please indicate the required format.

... by signing and returning this letter. The duplicate is for your ... you are the sole owner of the rights granted and that your ... copyright. If you do not control these rights, please ...

FIG 11.19
V shadow on a newspaper for pack shots.
"Another neat trick is to create controlled shadows over newspapers and magazines you are shooting for pack shots. This does two things it creates a more interesting shot and also draws the viewers eyes into the part of the page that you need them to look at. Simple but effective. Use colored gels to create another level of interest as well."

Take a look at the examples below where I have shown the difference between the same scene lit with the direct light and then soft light. It's a typical domestic location filming setup with the subject on a sofa and walls very close to the subject. In Figure 11.20 the photo shows a wide shot of the scene, which I've lit with a direct key light and backlight, and used the barn doors to keep any spill off the walls and the surrounding area.

FIG 11.20
Wider shot of the set than you would normally shoot.
"But it shows how the direct lighting is kept off the background areas which gives an intimate effect to the shot."

Figure 11.21 shows the same lighting with a mid-shot of the subject such as you would probably use for filming and the result is nice and clean with the subject standing out against the background and the small lamp on the table giving a pleasant affect to the shot (Figure 11.22).

FIG 11.21
So now when you frame a Mid shot the scene will look good.
"The key light is placed close to the wall and the barn doors are taking the spill light off the wall. It only works well if the key light is direct and does not have trace or spun on it. If it did have then a flag would be the only way to keep the spill light off the wall. The 3/4 backlight looks like it is coming from the table lamp over the subject's shoulder, which is just what we want. You could use the spill from the key light plus the backlight to illuminate the second guest and then be able to shoot a two shot without rerigging, saving time and effort."

If we change this direct key light to a soft light, a Diva 400W, then the effect on the wider shot will be shown in Figure 11.23. The soft light is spilling everywhere and the subject blends in with the background. It's the close background walls that are not helping and if there was a larger gap between the sofa and the walls, you could use this lamp effectively.

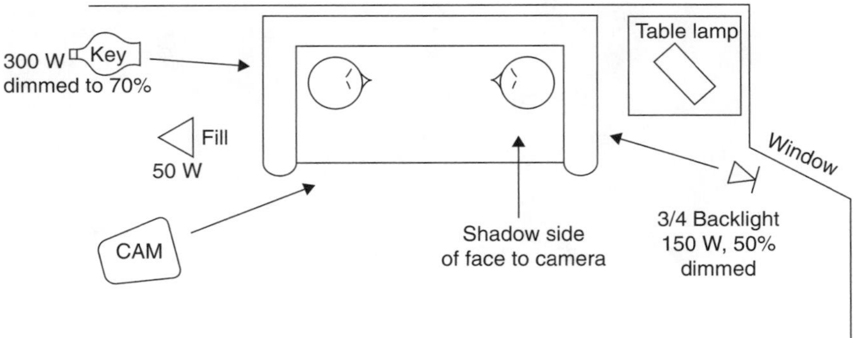

FIG 11.22 Lighting plot from above setup: direct light.

Figure 11.24 shows the mid-shot using the soft light above, and you can see that as the background has come up in light level; the feel of the whole shot has changed and the table lamp is much less prominent.

FIG 11.23 Soft light changes the scene.

FIG 11.24
And the Mid shot also looks different.

FIG 11.25
Soft light with egg crate in use.
"Now we have controlled the soft light and kept the spill off the wall the scene changes again but will still keep some shadow interest in the shot. Useful if you need to shoot female guests and do not want to use direct lighting."

To control the spill use an egg-crate or louver on the front of the lamp. It's doing a good job as the subject still stands out from the background and Figure 11.25 shows the final effect. You could lose even more spill by putting a flag in front of the Diva light to cut off the excess wall spill.

This effect is not so much of a problem if you are filming in a large location with the background farther away from your subject. Let's say your setup is in a large and roomy new office and you have the luxury of the guest being a long way from the background wall. You then have room to keep the camera away from the subject, zoom in, and get a better depth of field, but also you can use soft light without it falling on the background wall or sides of the shot. Thus this is an ideal situation.

SOFT LIGHT OPTIONS FOR LOCATION WORK

Kino-flow lights, seen in Figure 11.26, like the 400 W Diva lamp I used above, are good soft light sources for location filming as they are light, robust, and pack into a small carry case.

FIG 11.26
Kino Flow location light. "This is a 400 watt Diva version which gives a good output but is light enough to transport between locations."

The bulbs are similar in shape to fluorescent tubes but they are designed specifically for video and film shooting with correct color temperatures and other features. They are lightweight and durable, come in 200 W or 400 W combinations and 120 V or 230 V options, and have dimmers in line. To give you an idea of output, the Kino-flow 400 W is equivalent to an old Arri 2 K in power. You can use either tungsten balanced tubes for interior use or switch to daylight balanced tubes for exterior filming. Kino-flow also makes much larger versions of these lights as well.

The egg-crates or louvers come in 45, 60, and 90 degrees so you can concentrate the light onto your subject rather than it spilling everywhere. The 90 degree version gives a good modeling effect.

Chimera Softbank lights are also soft, shadowless lamp head boxes in various sizes and are a good workable soft light for location shooting.

For control you then use a soft black fabric grid over the front of the soft box to control the spill. These again come in 20, 40, 50 and 60 degree angles. See Figure 10.16 for a picture of the Chimera.

BOUNCED SOFT LIGHT

If you have enough space in your location room you can "bounce" your normal lights off photographic reflectors, white walls, or white boards. Suspend the reflector or board with another lighting stand and shine the lamp onto it so the reflected light hits your subject (Figure 11.27).

LIGHTING AN INTERIOR SCENE FROM OUTSIDE

Let's assume that you are shooting a corporate video on location and you have to light the inside of a small, ground floor office to give it the feel of daylight

FIG 11.27
Bounced light off of a reflector.
"The reflector is being held by a universal bracket which can accept many different sizes, this one is a 30 inch white reflector. It then clamps on top of a normal lighting stand and you can alter the angle and height safely. As always, it's about control."

coming through the windows and falling gently onto the actors inside. Now if you are filming multiple scenes in this location one aspect that will affect your decision about how to light it will be the fact that you are likely to have to move the camera many times as the action progresses, and if your lights are all inside with you it's going to be tiresome to change the lamps every time you need to alter the camera position.

However, a solution would be to create a base of light from outside, enough to give the room the right feel and level of illumination, and then supplement it with one or two lights inside to act as fill lights and backlights for the actors. That way you cut down on the amount of rerigging between takes as you will only be moving the two inside lamps. It's also a good way of ensuring that all the scenes you have filmed in the location have the same, consistent lighting to them. It will take you longer to rig the outside lights, but when done it should allow the shooting to continue throughout the day with less time being wasted and give a professional look (Figure 11.28).

FIG 11.28
"Outside lighting on a grand scale with 12/18 K HMIs going through trace frames before the windows but you can still achieve a good effect with smaller lamps."

TRACE FRAMES

Trace frames can also be used to provide useful light for other exterior filming jobs, and when powered by HMI-based lights they provide good soft illuminations for many purposes. HMI lights provide a light that is 5600 K and therefore matches in with most daylight situations. If you use two lamps through separate frames for two-handed interviews, you can achieve an effect of key light and backlight for both people by positioning the light and frames carefully. This means you could film with two cameras and only have to use two lights or use a single camera and not have to change lighting positions when you come to film the reverse shots (Figures 11.29 and 11.30).

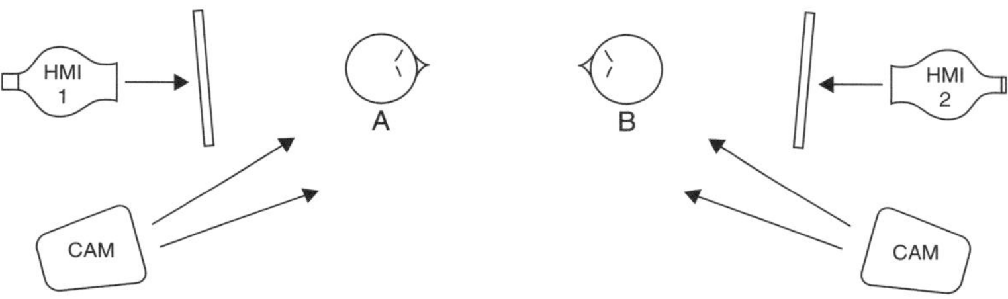

FIG 11.29
2× HMIs and 2× trace frames in positions.
"In this layout the light from HMI 1, going through its trace frame, is positioned high enough to act as a backlight on guest A as well as light guest B. The same applies for HMI 2. Both cameras should be able to get single shots and two shots of both people without seeing the trace frames in the side of shot."

FIG 11.30
Large set lit by Kinos.
"Of course there are soft light setups with small lights and there are soft light setups with lots of large lamps. This shot shows how a DOP/DP has lit a large area with soft top lights. They are all Kino-flows. He's now got a constant illumination to work with on the set and can then use floor standing lights to fill any subjects from the camera's point of view when they start shooting."

MATCHING THE EXISTING LIGHT

As I've mentioned before in Chapter 6, a lot of the lighting we need to do for real-world video shooting is based around using the existing interior light or daylight at the location we need to work in and finding a way to make it suitable for the project we are filming at the time rather than lighting everything from scratch. When it comes to matching existing light, there are four things to be considered:

1. **How bright is the light we have to match to?**
   If the light is extremely bright, say a sunny day outside, we will have problems matching this with a film light unless we have access to a powerful HMI light.

2. **What direction is it coming from?**
   Although the existing light might be fine, is it coming from the right direction and lighting the subject? If we need to work with a definite background, say it's a church because the presenter is referring to the church in his script and the light is from behind the church and subject, meaning both have their shadow side to the camera, it will mean using additional lights to light both elements or finding out if the sun hits the front of the church at some stage of the day.

3. **Is it constant?**
   If you have a long piece to film outside and you intend to rely on daylight then a day that has the sun going in and out between the clouds will prove very difficult for shooting. There are two solutions available to cope with this situation:
   - If you have no other choice than to film in these conditions you need to alter the iris manually every time the light changes.
   - The amount of iris adjustment will be dictated by the daylight changing on your guest.

And the only way to assess this is by keeping the viewfinder zebra on and using it as a meter, which will tell you how much to change the iris. Try and keep the same amount of zebra stripes apparent on your guest's face at all times; this will guide you to the correct exposure.

Secondly, you can use a film or video light, if you have one available and light your subject directly. If you light the subject so that he or she is correct for when the sun has gone in then you'll have a happy balance between both extremes as the sun will provide the main light source when it's out and the lamp will take over when the sun goes in.

4. **What color temperature is it?**
   Use the camera as a color temperature meter to find out what color the existing lights are before you start lighting with your video lamps. For instance, you might be shooting in a factory lit entirely by fluorescent strip lights. These can vary from tungsten 3200° and daylight 5600°. If you are unlucky enough to film under sodium lights it's even warmer than tungsten, making color balancing difficult (see Chapter 3 for more information about sodium lighting).

Once you have color balanced in the actual source available, you can decide which video lights to use, either normal tungsten lights or daylight-based HMIs, and what color correcting gels you need to match your film lamps to the conditions already there to the existing light.

HOW MUCH LIGHT TO USE?

If you overlight your subject compared to the background, the camera has to work at a smaller iris and the background will look darker than the subject. Conversely if you are faced with a background that is in bright sunlight and the subject is underlit compared to this the reverse effect will be apparent.

It's a good rule of thumb to try and balance the subject to the background; however, in the real world you could be left without any lights or a strong enough light to do this so other ways have to be found. In the case of the bright background, say an office block and subject in shadow, try the following. Scan the building to see if there are any dark or shadowy areas to be seen. Sometimes there are archways or covered areas that protrude and can be in shade. Reposition your subject in front of this area and there will be less difference between the two elements than before. The other way is to try and get the subject into daylight, again by repositioning him or her, but it's not always possible.

At nighttime you have a different set of challenges.

I normally use 3 dB of gain switched into the camera to try and get more information out of the background as the levels on the background are quite low. This means that I'm working at a wide f-stop, f2.0, and I've got a small depth of field so the background has gone slightly soft compared to my subject, which allows the subject to stand out. I've also used a battery lamp as a backlight. You can still make this work with only one or two lights by keeping the levels low on the subject, and this is a real-world solution as you might only have time to use the camera top light or one key light, perhaps. So if lightbulbs break or time is against you "go low" – you'll still achieve a good result for the final edit (Figures 11.31 and 11.32).

FIG 11.31
Shot of presenter in front of Big Ben London. with backlight on the side from the clock.
"In this shot the subject is lit by a small key light, 150W Dedo light. The 3/4 backlight is purposely coming from the same side as the illuminated clock face."

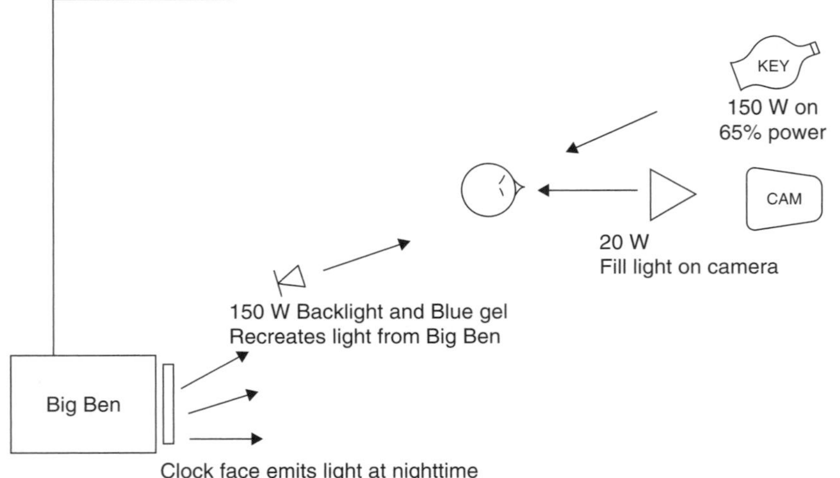

FIG 11.32
"Lighting plot of above setup."

If I had used a 650W lamp or an even larger one I would have had to stop down to about f5.6 and the background would be too dark to make out any significant detail within it. Also the backlight would not have been so effective as it would have been overpowered by the stronger front light.

CAMERA TOP LIGHTS

A lot of people disregard the humble top light and just assume its only use is for news cameramen, doorstepping celebrities, or politicians. Not quite so....

Obviously if the type of filming you do doesn't require a top light you'll probably not bother to have one on the camera. But many times this little lamp gets cameramen out of trouble and sometimes it can be a useful fill in lamp when you are using other floor lights. The reason why it's more important now than ever before is again down to the fact that modern cameras require less light level to work in as the chip CCDs they use to collect the light are faster than the cameras of a few years ago. This means that smaller wattage lamps can be used for lighting with far more affect and thus the humble camera top lamp comes into its own. From 20–50 W in power this light can be useful in many different ways (Figure 11.33).

TIP

When you are filming with tungsten lights (3200 K) you can try putting a blue gel on the backlight so as to get some color interest into the shot; this looks great on gray, light brown, or blonde hair .

FIG 11.33
Another way of using your camera top light. "I've taken my top light off the camera and placed to one side to get a better modeling effect on the subject."

LOCATION LIGHTING HEALTH AND SAFETY

It's always worth considering the safest way of working when using any electric powered film and video lights. In Chapter 15 there is more information relevant to location lighting safety, so have a look at that chapter and see how you can make your normal working routine even safer while filming on location.

I hope this chapter has helped sort out a few location lighting problems for you and also got your imagination working. Lighting is my favorite part of shooting, and the lights available now can achieve some great results. Never forget that good lighting can also be simple lighting; you don't need umpteen 12 K HMIs to make a scene look good. It's where the lamps are placed that is the key to good lighting. Finally, these rigs work with every camera from 35 mm film Arris, HDCAM's DVCAMs, and small palmcorders. I know, I've tried them all.

While I was researching this chapter, I was given a tour of Cirrolite in London by David Morphy, the MD. The lamp that impressed me most was an enormous beast that ran off a DC power pack the size of my bedroom wardrobe. This light provides 10 second bursts of very intense illumination but is totally flicker free. It is the largest battery lamp I've ever come across. I couldn't help wondering how useful it might be for my current day-by-day job of filming politicians in Westminster. The sheer joy of saying to some of the more long-winded MPs that they have only got 10 seconds to get their point over and then the lights go out would indeed be quite useful…Oh well, in my dreams I suppose….

CHAPTER 12

Cutaways, GVs, B Roll, Etc.

Cutaways, GVs, "B" roll, UPSOF, linking shots, generics…it seems that every TV station in the world has a different name for them but, call them by whatever name you will, they are the shots that go in between the actuality, and they can make a program, piece, or sequence look fantastic or look awful.

Some people say they are a black art conjured up by the devil himself, and many grown cameramen have been reduced to tears in many edit suites when it's all gone wrong…after the shooting has ended. So it's worth looking at this section of shooting and finding out what does work and what doesn't, because as location cameramen we spend an awful lot of our time shooting them one way or another.

Let's take two examples. Firstly what's your favorite sport?…When you watch it on TV how is the introduction put together? There is a very good chance that this intro/title piece is a combination of great music and graphics combined with nicely graded and treated live action shots, probably cut together quite quickly. These shots will be multilayered in the edit suite and have slow motion and speed ups with grainy colors and black and white efx put on it. These title sequences look more and more stunning as time goes on, such as mini pop promos or sections from video computer games, and they are there to draw the viewer into the show and they work fantastically well. For the program's producers they are vitally important, almost as much as the sport event itself.

But strip back this glossy finished product layer by layer and what do you come down to? Yep…a series of cutaways, well thought out, nicely shot with a specific look and style in mind, but they are still cutaways…

Then there are the big bucks documentaries often about natural history, wildlife, travel, and history. The well-known (and highly paid) presenter sets out on an epic trip of discovery to an unusual part of the globe with his film crew. His pieces to camera are filmed with camera cranes and steadicams against breath-taking backgrounds. After he's delivered his polished piece to camera, he walks off and there follows a voice-over section possibly with music. Look closely at these in between sections as the filming is normally exquisite. Long lens shots with a shallow depth of field giving a wonderful effect mixed with wide-angle shots, sometimes of huge panoramas and at other times with items tucked cleverly into the foreground to give more visual interest (Figure 12.1).

FIG 12.1
"Filming volcanic beach cutaways in Iceland on DigiBeta."

But they are still only cutaways…and exactly the same as many, many cameramen shoot after an interview or piece to camera for most of the normal filming day. Now we're probably talking about 35 mm film or HD cameras with lenses that cost a year's salary accompanied by multiple camera assistants for the examples above, but the same philosophy of shooting these shots can be transferred right down the camera food chain…DigiBetacam to Beta SP, SX

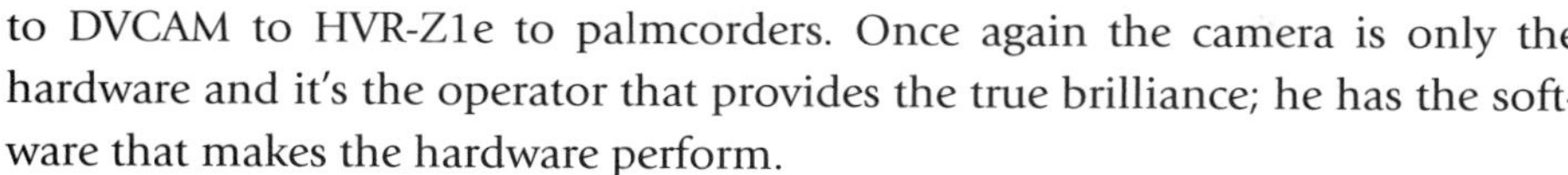

to DVCAM to HVR-Z1e to palmcorders. Once again the camera is only the hardware and it's the operator that provides the true brilliance; he has the software that makes the hardware perform.

The point I'm making here is that when you are out filming and you have to do the cutaways and GV's to go with the piece just filmed, you always have three decisions to make:

1. Shall I get these over and done with quickly with as little effort as possible?
2. Shall I make these shots really special and get them to add something to the show?
3. Shall I shoot lots of "in case" shots or shoot only the footage I need?

I told you they were funny little things, didn't I?

Now in the real world it's going to be difficult to shoot stunning shots like the ones I've been talking about all the time. This is partly because the high-end TV shows have location managers doing pre-shoot location research a long time before the camera? a long time before the camera gets there, so they know the best time of day to set up, which angle to get the best shot, and how the light will be falling when they get there. And for most of us for most of the time that's a real luxury we don't get given. But we can learn lots from looking at what shots are chosen for the final cut by the editor and director and the way that they are filmed and then cut into the final edit. In most cases you'll find one of the keys is to shoot a range of shots that are varied but are also relevant to the show and/or the main script.

Even if you are just starting out in camera work use this chapter to get an idea of what shots will work for the final cut or edit, possibly make a list of the ones that you find effective. Never mind that you may not know exactly how to shoot them, since you'll master "the how to do it" as you go on reading and shooting. But it's important to know what you want.

And if you make your living like I do, as a freelancer, then it pays off in the long run to keep your producers happy with varied and relevant cutaway shots that they can slot into their main pieces. At the BBC in London there are quite a few cameramen who have built well-deserved reputations this way, providing imaginative and creative shots that producers love to use in their shows. Even if the subject matter sounds a bit boring such as politics or economics, they still produce creative and imaginative work, and this pays.

When you are on location always bear in mind that the story or section that you've just shot could change as time goes on. If this is the case the editor will have to alter the final cut and want to use other shots, and if he doesn't have these at hand in the edit suite you'll end up reshooting. It's no one's fault but it does occur quite often. So when you are filming the cutaways, it's advisable to include a variety of different shots for this reason. Don't take this to mean shoot loads of extra shots that might or might not work; this just wastes time and is an excuse for not thinking and planning your cutaways. Well-planned shots will complement the script and bring extra life to the final piece and you do not need to overshoot to provide a variety of material.

My advice is to think about exactly the shots you need and go out to shoot these as well as possible but include some extra angles and viewpoints in case things change. This attitude will make you more choosy about your shots and push you to film them in a professional way (Figures 12.2–12.5).

It can also happen that an interview or section within a program simply doesn't work in the end edit, and if you've shot enough interesting and relevant

FIG 12.2

"Figures 12.2–12.5 have a short sequence of shots that you could shoot as cutaways for a piece on cars and transport. Instead of just filming the shots from one static position I've moved around to try and get some interesting angles and foreground. The last shot is purposely out of focus as I want it to be used as a mix out of the sequence. It could also be taken as a still frame, or slo-mo'd and text put over it."

FIG 12.3
This second shot shows the vehicles coming to a stop from another angle.

FIG 12.4
Always a good choice, tight shots of the action.

cutaways to help get around this unforeseen problem, the producers and the editor will be eternally grateful; it's helping them out and thats what counts.

If you are a beginner or coming into camerawork from, say, sound or production, keep reading from the example given in the following section, and if

FIG 12.5
A final shot that can be used to overlay graphics or simply to mix outfrom ends this series of cut-away.

you've got some experience jump ahead to where we start discussing the shots that matter and why they work and how they are done.

I'll start with an example to show how it could be done and after this is a list of what these shots have to do to work even for the humblest production with a small budget.

LOCATION SHOOT EXAMPLE

Mike and Jenny are shooting a documentary and one of the locations is Boston, by the river, in autumn. After 2 days of interviews and talking heads they have 1 day left to shoot the cutaways needed to complete the sequences already filmed. Each sequence will run to a maximum of 3 minutes when edited and the final cut comprises only the material they will shoot on location in Boston. There is no archive footage and no additional material to be used.

Mike gets up early, determined to get a good start and capitalize on the morning sun sweeping over the town's trees and river and giving that spectacular autumnal look that only New England can produce. He grabs the camera and leaves the hotel determined to shoot until late afternoon. He doesn't pack the script, story board, or running order and hasn't bothered to speak to the director, producer, or editor about the finished piece.

The light is perfect, no doubts at all, and he stays by the river shooting everything in sight. He gets so carried away with the beauty of the river that he does not cut tape at the end of every shot; sometimes he will just reframe, zoom in quickly on the new subject to refocus, zoom out, and hold it for about 8 seconds before repeating the process. Now and again he plays back the tape to check that it's all recorded OK but in his haste to get shooting again he doesn't requeue up the tape to the last frame he filmed (which you can do easily by pressing the return button on the lens). Mike knows that his shots will look spectacular as the river is just alive and sparkling through the viewfinder; his excitement is palpable…

Jenny approaches the task quite differently. She spoke to the producer, director, and editor the night before and asked a few questions about what they needed for the pieces. The director told her roughly which clips of the interviews from the past 2 days he wanted to use and gave her a brief note of what the interviewees had said in each one. Then he told her his ideas about how to link one interview to the next and what type of pictures would go well in this in between area. The producer said that she had wanted some shots of business- people going through the streets, which would work well to set the piece up. This could possibly be done on a very long lens and some out of focus feet shots so no faces were recognizable. If Jenny could get some reflections in the tall glass sky scrapers that would also be great, along with a few shots of old buildings. But other than that Jenny was to do what she thought would help the piece; some shots could be quite arty but with a mix of normal ones as well. Jenny already had notes from the editor asking for time-code to be sequential with no breaks as it was going into AVID and he did not want to lose precious time dubbing off rushes tapes that had broken code. He also said that if tapes came back with broken code and he had to use them the finished EDL would be a complete nightmare. Also he wanted two tracks of audio for all cutaways and GVs; the camera mic was fine.

As you may imagine Mike's shots came in and were great views of the river and life on the bankside but there was not enough other footages that could be used, so probably only a few shots would make the final cut. The rushes lacked any variety. As he had looked back at so many clips in the camera viewfinder but had not requeued the tape to the end of the last shot after viewing them he had two problems: (1) he had cut off the end part of shots already filmed, so many of them were too short to be useful. (2) This had also affected the time-code and there were gaps where the code would jump numbers, so the tape was now not sequentially coded. If the editor wanted to use a clip and the time-code jumped at the very start and at the end of the clip the editor could only choose a small section where the code was stable, again limiting the amount of Mike's shots that could be used. The whole tape would have to be dubbed onto a new tape, which would then give sequential time-code, but the problem of the shortened shots would still remain even after this. Mike had also only used one track of audio.

Jenny had slowly worked through her list of cutaways doing a variety of different angles and aspects at each different location. On some she had done a few wacky shots with canted head angles (camera tipped over to one side or the other) or very wide shots with movement in the foreground and the background. For crowd shots and businesspeople walking by she had filmed them as wide shots moving past the camera but then shot the shadows on the sidewalk produced by the long low sun, some of these she pushed out of focus to give an abstract image. It all looked very usable and probably 75% of her footage would be used with Mike's river shots making up the final 25%.

FIG 12.6
Wide shot over presenter's shoulders. "Choose a camera angle doesn't show the presenter's mouth moving, so the editor do which not have to worry about syncing the audio to the moving lips."

TIP
If you are shooting an interview with a presenter and one or more guests, to help the final edit it will normally be necessary to shoot some reverse cutaways, shots that can be used in the edit to shorten the piece or get in and out of tricky cuts. A wide shot of all the subjects plus presenter's reactions/noddies, and listening shots will be needed. For the wide shot try and do two separate angles: (1) from behind the presenter, just over his shoulder so that you can see the guests but not see the presenter's mouth moving, and make sure that the guests are listening but not talking on this shot. Zoom in and do a few tighter shots on each of them as well. (2) Over the shoulder and just behind the guests looking at the presenter using the same angle of view as you did on the presenter. Again get the presenter to listen and not speak, so it can cut and then zoom in and do tighter shots of the presenter that can be used as noddies (Figure 12.6).

WHAT SHOTS WORK

Let's move onto what cutaway shots work and how they are done.

Be relevant	It's no good shooting hours of what you think are great shots if they won't fit the subject matter or narration. Even if the subject matter or interview is on a dry and somewhat boring subject the cutaway shots need to be related to it and not just shots that you feel like shooting at the time. A good cutaway sequence adds to the script by highlighting the words with visuals. Keep focussed on what images will work. It can help to discuss the script or section with the director, producer, or editor beforehand as she will probably have an idea of what she wants.
Be varied	The camera can help the editorial content or script along by creative filming. Use a variety of different shots and movements to bring the subject alive. Use very wide shots, some with items in the foreground mixed with long lens shots with compressed depths of field. Use out of focus shots, use movement through the frame to pan with or tilt up and down with, use color and use shadow. Try canting the head (tilting the head and camera over at an angle) to get interesting takes on subjects.
Fade into the background	If you are in a busy area trying to get shots of people going about their daily business it can be difficult, as they can see you shooting them and will look straight at the camera or walk around you. Try turning the camera on to record and taking a step away from it slightly or reading a paper while standing next to it; people will not notice you so much. Remember to switch the front tally light (record light) off so you don't attract people's attention to the camera. But never invade people's privacy and if they ask not to be filmed then don't do it.

Plan	Plan, plan, plan. Great cut shots don't just fall into the viewfinder, they are – you've guessed it – planned. If you know that low evening light will give you better shots plan to be there then, not at midday.
Take a chance	Once you think that you've got enough shots done step back and think about a two or three other shots that would be a bit abstract or "off the wall" or really different. What I mean here is that after you feel the majority of cutaway shots that you need has been done do some other highly creative, unusual shots. It could be that you go in really tight on someone's eyes or shoot through the edge of the spectacles to give an abstract viewpoint. Possibly a handheld shot on a tight lens where the camera moves slightly. Defocussed shots and shadows on sidewalks work really well. Sometimes these shots work fantastically well in the final cut. But only experiment like this after you've got the routine shots covered. Don't rely on the wacky stuff to cover the whole section…unless it's a wacky shoot.
Use your imagination	Even the most normal day-by-day item can be made to look good with some thought. A bright colored item that is put into the side of a shot and pushed out of focus will give a shot an added dimension. An object filmed from an unusual angle can add visual interest. You are telling a story in pictures so use this as a tool to drive your choice of shots. People walking down a crowded street. Try filming their shadows, then push this out of focus and pan with the shadows. Tight shots of shoes and legs going through the frame can look stunning on the right day with the right light. And always look for contrasts in color, size, and subject. These types of shots work really well in the edit suite and can bring the most boring subject alive. In fact a really dry subject allows you to shoot abstract images which can look really good in the final cut.
Detail works: very tight shots cut in well	Try picking out detail shots in tight close-up. A sequence of tight or very tight shots often works really well in an edit. For example, if you are shooting a country cottage tight shots of window detail, door knockers, roof tiles, chimney stacks, and window boxes would make a nice sequence and match in well with the wide shots of the house. The tighter shots also show texture that will not be seen on wider shots.
Create depth in your shots	Creating some artificial depth works fantastically well on video. Positioning your subject so that you have other objects in the background will give more interest to your frames. Out of focus elements, patterns of light, shapes, and tones in the background all help the illusion of greater depth. Location shooters have the benefit of natural perspective and scenes to work with. And don't forget that some scenes will look better at different times of the day when perhaps the low light of dawn or sunset will give a better mood and feeling to the scenes.

How many shots do you need?	You need a crystal ball to answer this correctly as it all depends on the program/item/sequence you are filming. However, it's pointless shooting huge amounts of cutaways if your end piece only requires a few shots. Overshooting normally means you are filming "just in case shots" instead of shots that will work. Be focussed on what you want and need and get the best shots of these that you can. Quality is always far better than quantity, so think, plan, and then shoot what you feel fits the piece and make the shots as interesting as possible. When doing a pan across a subject, hold the shot for 15 seconds before panning and a good 15 seconds after you have finished panning, so the editor can choose these two static shots if needed and you don't have to film them separately. Always hold static shots for 10 seconds more than you think you need at the end of a record.
Audio	If you are working with a soundman he'll probably use a 416 mic or similar and get the correct audio and levels onto tape for you. But if you are working alone make sure you have the camera top mic switched on and the levels set manually, or, if you are happy with the auto setting, use this and forget about the audio from then on. If you don't have a top mic then use a separate mic, but always get some location audio from each place you shoot as the editor will need it to run under the shots.

TIP
If you've recorded your cutaways without any audio on them switch the camera to bars and record a further section with audio of the general location on it. This can then be used in the final edit or dub to run underneath your shots that do not have the audio on them and saves the editor searching for a section of sound that might do the job.

Some that don't work (see also "Video Editors Forum" in Chapter 8):

Bad framing	Poorly framed shots where the subject hides good backgrounds that would have added interest to the frame.
Shots that don't match the main action	If you have shot, the main action in a wide shot, it's worth doing it again, exactly the same, but with tighter shots. If you just get the actors or guests to mock up the action the chances are, unless they are professionals, that the movements won't match and will not cut in properly at the edit.
Too many wide shots	If you shoot only wide shots or shots that only vary in angle slightly it will be nearly impossible to cut as the action will jump about untidily on the screen.

Too low or too high	If you shoot your cutaways of presenters and guests from angles that are too low or high not only will they look ugly and unflattering but they probably will be hard to cut in as well.
Lighting that doesn't cut	If the main sequence has been shot in soft light don't overlight the cutaways or it will show on the screen. Always try to keep the main sequence lighting the same for the other shots needed.

There's a good chance that, whatever the subject matter of the piece you are filming, when the narration or voice-over starts, a wide shot of the scene, area, or subject will be useful. But instead of just plonking the camera down, zooming out wide, and recording what is in your immediate field of view, try to add a few more elements.

Foreground items work really well on wide shots.

A simple wide shot can be made twice as interesting with a foreground object included in it (Figure 12.7).

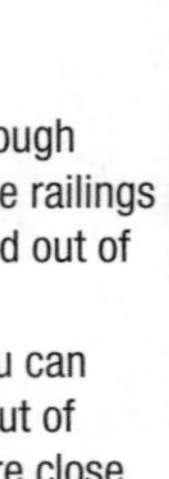

FIG 12.7
Parliament through Lambeth bridge railings with foreground out of focus.
"If possible you can try making it out of focus (if you are close enough), which gives an added depth to the shot; for example shooting through railings at your scene with the camera right up against the rails will give you a nice blurred foreground."

Same can be done with tree stumps, people, vehicles and Flowerstalls if they are fairly still (Figure 12.8).

FIG 12.8
Wide shot with flowers in the foreground.

You can try pulling focus from the foreground item to the background; this looks good.

If you then add another element, say, your presenter walking through the wide shot or movement from background objects then, it again adds interest to the shot (Figure 12.9).

FIG 12.9
Wide shot with foreground + person moving through the frame.

TIP

Sometimes it can be difficult to get the foreground in focus and the background out of focus enough, especially if you are working on a bright day and the camera needs to use a small iris. Try using an ND filter along with the back focus or macro lever, which is situated on the lens. Just adjust it enough to give you focus on the foreground object, which will throw the background out of focus (see Figures 12.10 and 12.11).

FIG 12.10
Macro lever in normal position.

FIG 12.11
Macro lever in switched in position.

It only works for static shots without zooms but it is very effective in giving you a shallow depth of field. Don't forget to put it back to its normal position when you've finished or you'll have problems keeping focus when zooming. Small prosumer cameras such as the SONY Z1 don't have this back focus facility but some have a macro switch/button.

GET MOVEMENT IN THE SHOT

A scene can be given more life with movement. So with the wide shots above try getting people to pass through the frame. If they do this close to the lens the editor can use this movement as a point to cut to, as it works like a wipe.

STATIC SHOTS AND PACK SHOTS

Finally a quick look at static shot cutaways that go into sequences. By this I mean shots of newspapers, magazines, static items, and ornaments that would be in rooms or offices. You might be asked to get a tight shot of an article in a newspaper or film a magazine with the pages being turned, perhaps it's a book or catalog. It's a simple request but as always you can choose to shoot and light it "straight" or put a bit of color and contrast into it to bring it alive. This is best shown in Figure 11.19, Chapter 11 where you can see an example of what I'm describing here. I've simply given the shot a bit of interest by lighting it with hard, shaped, shadowed light.

What you cannot see is that I've added color as well by keeping the camera on a preset tungsten filter and then using a blue gel over the lamp (if you can see the blue color please get in touch with me…I'm worried). On location I often make the shadow profile out of two bits of cardboard from old tape boxes that are lying around; clip them together with lighting clips; sometimes known as "croc" clips; and use a second lighting stand to hold them in place. Then you simply adjust the shadow by moving it nearer or closer to the subject. The shape can be varied; you can probably use preformed shapes purchased from photographic shops or film lighting companies, but this way is quite effective if you want a simple shadow shape. It only takes a bit of time but I'm always surprised by the number of editors and producers that come up after the edit and thank me for these simple shots.

CHAPTER 13

News and Current Affairs

Every country in the world seems to have numerous TV news stations and 24 hour rolling TV news is commonplace. Running alongside these many news shows are hosts of web sites going into further detail about each item and story of the day and are updated frequently. Both the TV and web sites have a voracious appetite for pictures and content to fill them, and video work varies from straightforward news gathering, quick interviews, live hits, doorstepping politicians, and covering press conferences to high-quality, stylish interviews and setups (Figures 13.1 and 13.2).

This sector of work, along with current affairs filming, probably employs more cameramen and, women per day across the globe than any other type of shooting and as it's all location-based work we'll take a look at how best to approach it from an operator's point of view (Figure 13.3).

News and current affairs camera work used to be seen as the poor relation of TV shooting but that's simply not true any more. Most stations have different types of filming to be done from shooting clips, packages, and sequences in order to tell a complete news story to location shooting for flagship current affairs shows that will most probably have an in-house style for interviews that they want replicated by all cameramen and will have high production values.

We'll look at how to cover both requirements quickly and effectively with today's video cameras.

FIG 13.1
In 2007 the build up to Gordon Brown becoming the new U.K. Prime Minister drew many news crews from all over the world to number 10 Downing street. Unless you've actually shot here, it's hard to explain what a small cramped street Downing street is, and how cold it can get, yet I counted over 70 different TV crews and 90 photographers at the change of the Prime Minister. Purpose built platforms were rigged to hold the many live points and crews for different stations.

A common list of camera work to be done by most stations would be as follows:

- Day-by-day news gathering on location including 1 + 1 recorded interviews.
- Press packs events, where many photographers and cameramen are in a scrum to cover a popular event or breaking news story.
- Press conferences for one-man bands.
- Live hits into scheduled programs.
- Sequences and packages filmed for specific news stories or current affairs items.

I imagine that different news stations around the world call some of these jobs by other names but the actual work will probably be the same.

FIG 13.2
The power of TV never ceases to amaze me.

FIG 13.3
The most famous front door in Britain, number 10 Downing street, home to the Prime Minister and about 170 stills and video crews for 1 day in 2007.

DAY-BY-DAY NEWS GATHERING ON LOCATION

News gathering, ENG, and PSC (Figure 13.4) all mean recording specific jobs on a single camera and nine out of ten times will be on location. For this type of work you can use many types of video camera, from DigiBetacam down to SONY Z1es, and if you doing freelance the chances are you'll either have your own kit or use the kit provided by the stations employing you. Here in London at the Westminster's Millbank building there are five major TV stations: BBC, SKY, ITV, ITN, and Channel 5. And there is a complete mix of different formats and cameras. BBC uses DVCAM, SKY uses SX, ITV uses SP Beta and DVCAM, and ITN uses Panasonic DVCAM pro. I think everyone has SONY Z1es as well, and at least two stations are moving to Panasonic's P2 format.

But as I have said earlier in the book it's not about what camera you use but about how you use it and what you do with it that matters.

By their very nature, news stories tend to be last minute items and sometimes very little planning can be done before the shoot. It's normally a case of, "Hi, we need to shoot X, Y, or Z within the next 10 minutes so grab the kit and let's go." In fact most requests from news organizers to news crews are unreasonable as there's never enough time to get prepared but that is the environment of news and you have to understand this mindset if you're going to succeed in it.

FIG 13.4
All makes of ENG Video cameras ready for the next news event in London.

So the first practical solution for crews to cover this is to have all their kit, prepared, ready to go, and close at hand. And the first rule of news camera work is always, always have a tape/card/disk inserted in the camera before the next job happens. Even when walking out to the job or from the car park, make sure it's loaded as you never know when you will need to roll to record.

Taking this one step further, it's a good idea to have recorded bars for about 10 seconds on the front of every new tape before you get to the location. This does two things: it proves to you that the tape is working and that a signal is being recorded before you need to film your job. If the tape has a problem, it could be overtensioned, buckled, or the camera heads might be dirty; then most cameras will flash up a warning light and you'll know to sort it out, before getting to your next job. Secondly the editor will use the bars to line up the recorded tape on his edit deck.

The second rule is that the camera microphone needs to be switched on at all times in case you need to grab the camera and film what is happening and being said at a moment's notice. That's why many news cameramen keep one channel of audio on auto and switched to camera mic in between jobs; that way they don't waste any time fiddling with buttons and switches before recording; they simply switch the camera on, throw it on their shoulders, and hit the red button.

It's also why news cameras always have camera top lights, because they only need one button to illuminate the subject, saving time. No one wants to miss the shot or waste valuable shooting time because a button was in the wrong position or the tape had a problem or you were rigging a light.

Many news crews are one-man bands nowadays, so the next practicality is deciding what kit and how much of it you take to everyday jobs. So with the camera and tripod on each shoulder, extra microphones, lights, batteries, tapes, gels, and leads have to live in a rucksack or a similar bag.

A typical kit of a one-man band video kit is shown in Figure 13.5.

FIG 13.5
Typical kit and accessories that can be used for news, current affairs and interviews. Not too heavy and extra kit can supplement it as needed, like radio mics, desktop mic stands and other items. Whether you are using a ENG kit or HVR-Z1e, there are crucial items that you will always need with you on a shoot.

If you have a camera top light as standard then an additional light such as a lightweight Sachtler reporter 300W, classic Dedo, or Arri 150/300 can just about be carried in a rucksack or by hand. This gives you the option of using the extra lamp as a key light to give your subject some modeling and the camera top light should do a good job of filling in the eyes and mouth, giving you a well-lit shot. To balance the two lights, use a dimmer or ND filter on the key light so it does not overpower the fill light. The lighting balance between the two lights is working correctly when you can just see the fill light lifting the shadow areas on the face when the key light is switched on (Figure 13.6).

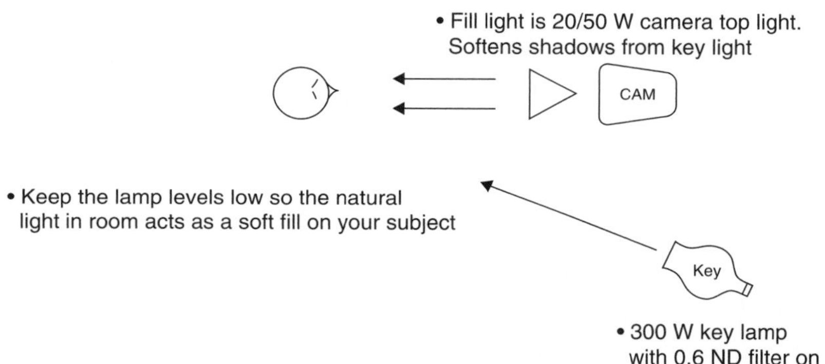

FIG 13.6
With the subject lit by the key light, the camera top light becomes an effective fill light as it's coming from the same height as the lens. The main thing is to get a correct balance between the two lights with the fill light working at no more than 50% of the key light's illumination. So even news shots can be carefully lit and look good. There's no excuse for bad lighting these days.

Lamps of 650W and over are normally too heavy to carry any distance unless you can get another person to help with the load.

OTHER TIPS FOR EVERYDAY NEWS GATHERING

When Shooting 1 + 1 Interviews or News Gathering

When shooting 1 + 1 interviews or news gathering, find out whether the editor or producer needs setup shots and cutaways in order to complete the package. If these are needed, then make sure the setup shot lasts for a minimum of 10–15 seconds. Anything shorter may leave the editor without enough length of shot to match to the voice-over, especially if this audio has to be longer than normal in order to explain the story to the viewer. Also make sure that the setup shot is relevant and the location you are shooting in works for the script. I always shoot one or two general cutaways without the subject or journalist in frame; it could be a shot of the background building used for the interview, for example, so the editor has this if the script changes. And a few reaction shots from the presenter along with a wide two shot from over the guest's shoulder normally helps in the edit as well. See Chapter 12 for more on location cutaways.

As always with news and current affairs the main enemy is time, or the lack of it, so you need to judge how much you can shoot in the time given to you. A few well-planned shots are better than a large bunch of shots that have been rushed and don't relate to the subject matter.

Press Packs and Breaking News Events

Press packs and breaking news events, where many photographers and cameramen are in a tight scrum to cover popular events can be a real nightmare (Figures 13.7 and 13.8).

FIG 13.7
Press packs small and large, 90% waiting around, 10% frantic activity. But if you didn't get there early enough to grab a good position then your shots won't be the ones that get on air.

Depending on how well they have been organized by the events PR department or press company, these shoots vary from pleasurable to outrageous, and you normally won't know until you get there. If, like the Downing Street event in the photo, it's been well thought out, then podiums for camera crews, lamps,

FIG 13.8
Multiple tape and hard disk formats are used in Current affairs and news gathering world wide.

power, distribution amplifiers (DA), running audio through an XLR socket and a mixing desk will be provided making it relatively easy to get good pictures and audio. Other events, though, will have nothing available for the crews who are left to fight it out amongst themselves.

No matter what camera you are using to shoot on the main problem is the same, how to get the best, usable shots and audio in tight, uncontrollable conditions.

Take only the kit you need and no more; if there are many crews in a small area then work without a tripod, if you can, as you will be more mobile and be able to change positions faster. A small set of steps will be useful if you need to shoot over the heads of other crews, and enough batteries to last the length of the shoot is a must. If you are a one-man band, then the audio can be difficult, especially if you find yourself at the back of the pack. You'll need to keep one channel of audio switched to the camera microphone to catch the entire atmosphere and any direct speech from the people near the camera. The chances of getting a microphone near your subject could be slim if everything is all happening in real time, but I always take a handheld radio microphone with me on these occasions as you might find someone nearer to the subject who'll point it in that direction while you shoot.

Many events will now arrange a set of audio feeds for crews so look around for a distribution box and take a spare XLR lead so you can plug into it. Always work out what audio level this box is outputting; it's normally either line level or mic level, and adjust your camera's audio settings to it. Line level comes in at 0 dB whereas mic level comes in at −60 dB. If you don't monitor the feed and adjust your camera to the correct setting, you can find the incoming audio is distorted and this will then go down to tape/disk as you record.

A few times I've grabbed an audio feed from a friendly sound recordist who is using a boom to get over the heads of other crews. This works fine and also highlights an important point about managing relations with other crews. It pays dividends to be friendly and helpful to all other crews on these jobs. The guy or girl who helps someone out one day will be the person who is helped the next day. If you let a crew have your spare battery because they are desperate for the one last shot to get their job done, then there's a good chance that they will give you an audio feed when you are desperate for sound on the next event. Another way to get good audio if you are stuck at the back of a hall is to place your radio microphone next to or on a PA speaker, then you can feed it straight into your camera.

As a whole most news and current affairs crews from around the world face the same problems day in and day out and any help when needed is always gratefully received. If you work with a journalist or a presenter, then life can be easier as you can get them to hold the microphone near to the action for you. Always get some cutaways of other crews filming and action away from the main scene to help cut the piece. See the wish list of shots in the section below as they relate to this kind of shoot.

Press Conferences for One-Man Bands

Press conferences for one-man bands can again be difficult to cover as you are dependent on how well, or not, they are organized. I'm now referring to organized conferences, mostly indoors, and with people seated and taking questions and giving answers. The problem here is how to get good audio from a group of people who are spread out. Hopefully you will be able to access an organized sound feed like in the example above. But just in case they don't supply one it's worthwhile taking a handheld radio microphone and a small desktop mic stand along.

If you get stuck with a bad camera position far away from the podium or audio DA box, then you can place your radio microphone on the podium and get really good sound. The other benefit is that with this rig you can shoot cutaways and move around the room at will, changing angles and shooting a good variety of shots with sound being laid down all the time and no restrictive cables holding you back. If the group is very spread out try using the handheld radio mic on the desk or podium as above but also using your interview microphone on a long XLR cable as well. This way you can split the microphones onto separate audio tracks and get sound from both sides of the group. Most cameras will allow you to monitor both channels of audio so you can alter the levels as you need to.

Finally it's always a good idea to try and get some cutaway shots of something other than the main table or speakers. Good editing shots include:

- Shots of the audience, photographers, and cameras, and if you can grab a shot from behind the main table and with some of the main people in the foreground this also works well.
- Shots of people writing, tight hands and pens.
- Shots of people on the main table when they are not speaking and looking toward the speakers.
- If the event is based on the presentation of a report or document get some shots of this, the front cover, and possibly a reader reading through it and turning pages.
- Always get a wide shot of the exterior of the building where the event is being held or if you can't then a wide shot of people going into/out of the room.

LIVE HITS INTO SCHEDULED PROGRAMS

Live hits into scheduled programs are becoming more commonplace jobs for video camera crews over the world. As the need for live inserts to TV shows grows and becomes more popular and the technology becomes easier to work with, location camera crews working in news and current affairs can expect to come across jobs like these at most TV stations. There's now a few ways that locations can be used as live transmission points: through the use of purpose installed injection points that simply need video and audio plugging into them, through Sat trucks that take both signals from the camera crew into the truck and then handle the transmission and return clean feed audio to the crew, and through computer and mobile phone technology allowing software to handle signals and play through the Internet and networks.

The injection points are normally found in places such as halls and public areas that are frequently used by TV stations as stand-up points for live transmissions. Not surprising, really, as they take a lot of setting up and cable laying to get them operational. But the basic way of working is the same the world over. The camera connects its video signal either through the "video out" BNC connector or has a separate SDI output on the camera. This connects to the inject point in the wall box. Sound would come from the sound recordist's audio mixer and again go into the wall box. The return video from the gallery of the show would come into the wall box and then go into the sound mixer where it would be split and sent to the presenter and also the cameraman, so they can both hear the program and any instructions from the gallery, and the presenter or guest can hear the questions and take part in any debate. The sound recordist can control:

- the level of audio from the guest going to the studio;
- the level of incoming audio/clean feed from the studio to the guest;
- the level of audio to the cameraman.

And with these controls in place the crew can work in the location, taking instructions from the studio and altering any shots and requirements as needed. They can use the presenter's microphone to talk directly to the studio. Mains power would also normally be available from the injection point as well.

It's possible to alter the rig so that a one-man band can do the job with audio coming out of the camera, but you need to make sure that balanced audio can be fed from the camera you intend to use and a method of hearing the studio's clean feed is available as well. Sat trucks provide the link between the studio and location crew and can also mix two cameras into one signal for certain shoots. They act as the conduit for all signals and communications between the crew and the TV station's gallery.

Tips for filming lives include:

- Always try and run off the mains power. If you do have to run off batteries have a second battery standing by, preferably sitting in a holder that can plug straight into your camera's DC socket. This way if you see the onboard camera battery getting low, you can just plug this second battery in without having to take the first one off and it shouldn't affect the picture output as it's being plugged in. PAG make a good flying lead that you attach the battery to one end and camera mains socket at the other end. IDX batteries that can be "piggy backed" together to provide power for a longer period are needed.
- Have the camera top light plugged in and ready to go. If your main light has a problem and suddenly switches off while you are on air then you can quickly switch the camera lamp on to take its place.

- It's also useful to a have a small mirror and a powder compact containing neutral foundation in your bag in case the talent/presenter has forgotten hers. She'll be so relieved if you have one and you'll create a great impression.

Sequences and Packages

Sequences and packages filmed for specific news stories or current affairs items can be where the cameraman can show some creative input. The producer will be looking for interesting ways to illustrate the story and add value to the reporter's script. It's not as easy as it first looks because you have to get the whole story told in a set amount of time and this can vary from 30 seconds to a few minutes depending on the show's running order. But if he want a package running for 30 seconds it's no good providing a final cut that goes to a minute just because there were some great shots that might look good. The art in these jobs is to get it all shot and edited in time. No longer time than the slot you are shooting for is allowed so that the audience can understand the story and take in the facts. A lot of mistakes in shooting these jobs can be avoided by finding out what shots work and what ones don't before shooting begins, and a good source for this information is video editors. Have a look at Chapter 8, the section titled "Video Editor's Forum," where there is a list of comments by editors that apply to cameramen shooting these sequences. It's all real-world information that is helpful to us all. If we break down the components within each package it reads like this:

- Setup shots
- Pieces to camera by presenter
- Voice-over/narration
- Interviews with people involved in the story
- Cutaway/GV shots to illustrate narration and pieces to the camera – shoot a variety of tight shots and wide shots so the editor has a good choice
- Detail/pack shots as needed

All of the above can be done in camera and you'll find information on each part throughout the book. Even the voice-over can be done well on location if you use a car or hotel room and take care. See Chapter 5 for how to do this.

CHAPTER 14

Location Filming Abroad

An important part of the joy in single camera filming is being able to fly off somewhere new to film. Video kits are now quite lightweight and this makes traveling easier. But no matter how light the gear and how exciting it is to nip off to foreign countries, you will need to be prepared for added problems as you go about your shooting (Figure 14.1).

Proper planning can help sort out many problems before you get there. If your shoot is for a separate production company, they will look after many of the items needed to be arranged such as sorting out locations, booking flights, hotels, and transport. But if you are working alone at least some of these jobs will fall to you to arrange and there can be a surprising amount of work to be done.

After being a cameraman for many years I had the opportunity to direct and produce a TV series with my partner John Wilson, who was a writer/presenter. This series was called "Go Fishing" and we traveled to many parts of the world filming fishing and adventure programs. On the very first shoot I managed to book all the crew into a great hotel and sorted out a deal to get everybody into upgraded rooms, which they loved. However, I also managed to forget to book a room for John and myself, so we had to share the hotel's spare guest room, which was next to the kitchen and used to store empty beer barrels and cans. I've never known a crew laugh so much when they heard, but I had to admit it was funny and I never made the same mistake again. I now always work from a list.

So if it falls to you to do the organizing and you would like to avoid my unique mistakes then here are a few tips to help it go smoothly.

FIG 14.1
Shooting a feature for GMTV in Iceland.

- Always work according to a list of *production jobs to be done* and start with the most difficult tasks first, as these will probably be the ones that take the most time to resolve. Things such as contacting people or agencies you have never met before and asking for permissions or facts can take up much more time than you expected.
- Table 14.1 has a list of production filming planning requirements; just cherry-pick the ones that apply to your particular shoot and use them to help get set up. Your list can be tailored to fit the type of shooting you do most or countries you need to visit for shooting, so it becomes relevant to you and a lot of the information can be reused on subsequent trips. Make up your own version as a spreadsheet document for added speed and budget control.
- If you want even more financial control over your program and shoot budget produce another Excel document with all the headings and budget amounts and take it one step further by turning this into a cash flow document for the entire time of the shoot starting at the planning and research stage and ending at the delivery of the final product.
- If you've never done this before, the aim is to look at each budget heading and the amount you have allocated to it and then forecast when the money will be available for this section and then estimate when you will be

Table 14.1 Location Filming Abroad Planner

Job/task	Detail/£	To be completed by	Tick when done
Travel			
■ Arrange flights ■ Cost? ■ Arrange taxi to/from airport ■ Cost? ■ Arrange transit to/from hotel ■ Cost? ■ Arrange Car-hire ■ Cost? ■ Arrange taxis for location ■ Cost? *Total cost travel*			
Accommodation ■ Arrange hotels ■ Cost? *Total cost accommodation*			
Crew hire *Cameraman* ■ Cost/day ■ Cost/total *Second cameraman* ■ Cost/day ■ Cost/total *Soundman* ■ Cost/day ■ Cost/total *Electrician* ■ Cost/day ■ Cost/total *Video editor* ■ Cost/day ■ Cost/total *Total cost crew hire*			
Production team hire *Production manager* ■ Cost/day ■ Cost/total			

(*Continued*)

Table 14.1 *(Continued)*

Job/task	Detail/£	To be completed by	Tick when done
Assistant producer			
■ Cost/day			
■ Cost/total			
Researcher			
■ Cost/day			
■ Cost/total			
Office assistant			
■ Cost/day			
■ Cost/total			
Location manager			
■ Cost/day			
■ Cost/total			
Runner			
■ Cost/day			
■ Cost/total			
Total cost production team hire			
Shooting kit			
Camera			
■ Cost/day			
■ Cost/total			
Second camera			
■ Cost/day			
■ Cost/total			
Spare batteries			
■ Cost/day			
■ Cost/total			
Extra lenses			
Wide-angle adapter			
■ Cost/day			
■ Cost/total			
Remote zoom control			
■ Cost/total			
Lights			
■ Cost/day			
■ Cost/total			
Dollies			
Steadicam			
Extra grip equipment			
■ Cost/day			
■ Cost/total			

(Continued)

Table 14.1 *(Continued)*

Job/task	Detail/£	To be completed by	Tick when done
Sound kit ■ Cost/day ■ Cost/total			
SQN mixer ■ Cost/day ■ Cost/total			
416 ■ Cost/day ■ Cost/total			
2× ECM 77 *Radio hand mic* *Radio personal mics* ■ Cost/day ■ Cost/total			
Extra sound gear ■ Cost/day ■ Cost/total			
Drop-proof cases ■ Cost/day ■ Cost/total			
Total cost filming kit			
Insurance ■ Cost/total			
Equipment list Carnet ■ Cost/total			
Subsistence *Meals for crew per day* ■ Cost/total			
Postproduction *Edit suite hire* ■ Cost per day ■ Cost/total			
Sound dubbing ■ Cost per day ■ Cost/total			
Copies and dubs ■ Cost/total			
Delivery and transport ■ Cost/total			

spending it. This might sound like a pedantic way to work but it will force you to take control of the income and payments of each budget heading and is the key way to keep a production budget under control. After all, you are probably putting a lot of time and energy into the filming and editing, so the last thing you want is for the budget to all be spent before the job is done.

Anyone who has produced a program for outside TV stations will probably have had to create a cash flow sheet. Look at Table 14.2 where I've laid out a simple cash flow sheet for a typical shoot. This will allow you to see when the main costs occur so that you can arrange the cash in time for payments. As you progress with the production you simply enter the true costs in the place of these forecast costs. Then you can see if you are over or under budget for different sections and you can make decisions based on this.

- Work out how long you think it will take to plan and set up the trip and shooting, then double it so you have some time in hand to change things when you've finished or something alters along the way.
- If it's a complicated filming trip involving lots of people, many locations, and various crew members and possibly actors, then get the help of a qualified production manager. He can help you set up the trip and will have a good idea what permissions, costs, and administrative matters will be in different countries. He will also be able to advise you from day one of the planning, and this will help speed up the process of preproduction. If the job is complex then he can oversee the different stages with you and keep a check on the budget, then at the end of the job he will tidy up the loose ends and summarize the budget position for you. He can also take control of the budget and cash flow for you leaving you free to concentrate on the shoot.
- If you don't use a production manager then get someone else to double-check your list when it is completed. Another set of eyes can pick up mistakes and problems faster than your own. You'll find that as you have been so engrossed in the work that simple things might have been left out. And the item most people have forgotten about, at least once in their careers, is to buy, collect, or pack the tape stock. And always find out where you can purchase new stock in the area you intend to film as you might find that the stock box gets mislaid by the airline or some similar problem. Or like myself you could famously leave the tape stock sitting on top of your car roof in the car park at 0400 in the morning whilst you and the crew motor out 20 m from the shore to film a fishing trip...which we then had to do with the one tape that was in the camera....

Table 14.2 Budget and Cash Flow Planner for Location Shoot

Budget headings... Celebrity news shoot, Paris	Budget £	January	February	March	April	May	Totals	Totals	Over/ under budget	Percentage difference
Preproduction										
Labor costs										
Director/ Producer/ Research Assistant	4000.00	3000.00	1000.00					4000.00		
Research costs								0.00		
Research travel costs	1000.00	250.00	750.00					1000.00		
Research hotel costs	800.00		800.00					800.00		
Research subsistence	300.00		300.00					300.00		
Production costs								0.00		
Crew labor								0.00		
Director	2000.00			1000.00	1000.00			2000.00		
Cameras	1500.00			750.00	750.00			1500.00		
Sound	1500.00			750.00	750.00			1500.00		
Ground costs while on location	1000.00			500.00	500.00			1000.00		

(Continued)

Table 14.2 *(Continued)*

Budget headings... Celebrity news shoot, paris	**Budget £**	**January**	**February**	**March**	**April**	**May**	**Totals**	**Totals**	**Over/ under budget**	**Percentage difference**
Hotel costs for crew	1200.00			600.00	600.00			1200.00		
Travel costs for crew	700.00			350.00	350.00			700.00		
Local taxi travel	300.00			150.00	150.00			300.00		
Subsistence for crew	600.00			300.00	300.00			600.00		
Camera kit	1100.00			500.00	600.00			1100.00		
Sound kit	950.00			400.00	550.00			950.00		
Lighting kit	450.00			350.00	100.00			450.00		
Tape stock	200.00			100.00	100.00			200.00		
Postproduction costs								0.00		
Director costs for off-line and final edit	1000.00					1000.00		1000.00		

Total edit package inc editor and kit	970.00					970.00		970.00
Sound dub costs								0.00
Director	300.00					300.00		300.00
Sound studio costs	600.00					600.00		600.00
Voice-over artists	300.00					300.00		300.00
Graphics: Total package								
Contingency	500.00			100.00	100.00	300.00		500.00
Totals...Running horizontally	21,270.00	3250.00	2850.00	5850.00	5850.00	3470.00	21,270.00	
Totals...Running vertically								21,270.00

Tourist boards based in the country and area that you intend to film can be a great help and source of information. They are there to help promote the area and have a wealth of knowledge about locations, accommodation, travel logistics, etc. And most will have dealt with film crews before and have some experience of what is needed.

So if you need to set up a few good GVs and wide shots to set the scene for your shoot they should be able to advise you where the best places are, how to get there, and what time of day to film for the best light and where a good view point will be. How far the place is from your hotel, parking restrictions and costs, hire car or taxi fees, and likely tips can also be discussed with them, so you'll be able to keep a good grip on that old filming budget in your back pocket.

They can also suggest other web sites with pictures of other locations that might be of use to you. From this info you can start plotting your daily filming schedule.

If your shoot will help showcase the local area and be of benefit to tourism then you can see whether the tourist board has a budget available to help with your ground costs. But you must be honest with them and explain exactly where and when your finished program will be shown and what the likely audience figures will be. If you have the rights to the finished show you might be able to offer the tourist board some use of the end product, so it can use it for promotion if can help with the costs. Again it's a way to help get the best out of your visit and keep costs to a reasonable level. On our international fishing programs the tourist boards were extremely useful and helped with many little problems that we could not have dealt with ourselves.

When you plan the filming day in a foreign country, never make it too tight as the chances are that you will work slower than you normally do. Leave some extra time in the day so that any problems getting to locations or guests being late for shooting don't leave you running out of time or cause the day's schedule to be wrecked.

Many countries will have some types of rules and restrictions for film crews to adhere to. For instance, if you come across to London and want to film around the city and/or if you are near the political area known as Whitehall, you might not know that it is not allowed to use a tripod on the pavements but that you can film with handheld cameras. Now you might get away with using your tripod, especially if it's a quiet time of the day or not too crowded, but be careful in busy times, or they will accuse you of causing an obstruction. And the nearer

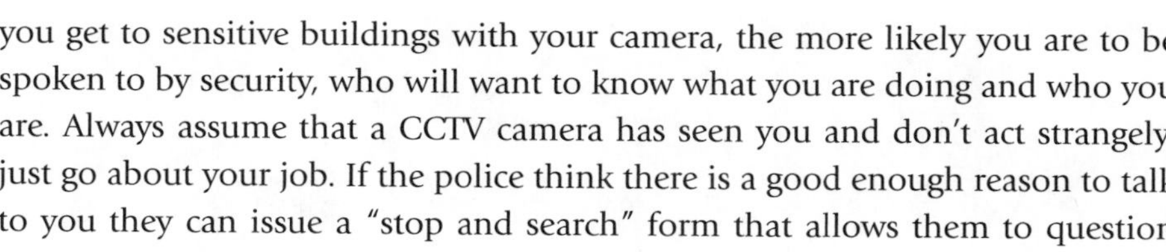

you get to sensitive buildings with your camera, the more likely you are to be spoken to by security, who will want to know what you are doing and who you are. Always assume that a CCTV camera has seen you and don't act strangely, just go about your job. If the police think there is a good enough reason to talk to you they can issue a "stop and search" form that allows them to question you on the spot.

The best way of being allowed to get on with your work in these cases is to always carry a press pass with you along with one other form of photo ID, and make sure they are current and have not expired (Figure 14.2). In every country I've filmed this card has always got me out of trouble. You can get a press card through your company if you are staff or through your craft union if you are freelance or self-employed. If you are intending to shoot specific private buildings such as those occupied by large companies contact their press department before shooting and arrange for permission to do the shots. Even if you only need to do a quick 20 in. shot of the outside, it's best to let them know beforehand and avoid longwinded explanations to the doormen. This way you can have a name and contact and if questioned by security you can quickly get on with the job. A letter from someone inside the organization giving you permission to shoot around their premises always helps iron out security problems. It's also a good way to make useful contacts for the future should you want to use that company premises again. Never miss an opportunity to network in this business; it can be a lifeline.

Your union or craft organization might also be able to advise you about filming in other countries and it should be able to contact its colleagues in the country you intend to go to for information that will help.

FLYING WITH YOUR KIT

It used to be the case that airlines welcomed crews aboard and happily allowed you to use a spare seat to strap your camera in. The reality now is that restrictions on all hand luggage and draconian security checks in all airports mean that flying with a kit is a challenging prospect. Flying with kit a comes down to two choices: take the camera on board or put it in the hold in drop-proof boxes. Most airlines now allow a maximum of only one or two items of hand baggage to be taken on board, and if this includes your camera you'll have to be prepared to put it in the overhead lockers. So make sure that the size and weight of your case will fit in the locker by contacting the airline first and talking it through. It's worthwhile making this call anyway because you might be

FIG 14.2
Paul's press pass and ID.

able to get an agreement to take the camera and a personal hand item through together. Once again you'll make a new contact in the airline, which will be very useful if you run into trouble when traveling and need to quote this person's name to smooth things over, and secondly you might need to talk to the airline again in the future; all well worthwhile.

If you are taking an ENG camera fitted with a battery and lens you can try breaking it down into two smaller hand cases, one for the lens and battery and one for the lens, but you'll have to give the second bag to another crew member to carry on.

Always have a fully charged battery available when taking the camera through customs and security as there is a 90% chance they will want to see it switched on and working before allowing you through.

FLYING WITH LITHIUM BATTERIES

Airlines now have new policies in place for flying with lithium batteries, which will affect crews traveling abroad. New regulations cover lithium ion batteries and you will need to have a statement of conformity from the maker of the battery, which will show how much lithium is contained in the battery unit. If you take them as hand luggage then they will need to be in a sealed container.

RADIO MICROPHONES ABROAD

Before flying check to make sure you know which radio mic frequencies the country you are filming in uses. U.K. licensed radio mics use channel 69 but in America this is kept for emergency use; you won't impress many people if you are using this frequency and a fair bit of explaining will be in order.

Many cameramen do not like the thought of putting their camera into the airline's hold for two reasons – it might get damaged and it might get on the wrong plane and end up somewhere you are not present. Some airlines have a policy of not allowing heavy hand baggage in the plane so if you are using a heavy camera and it is too heavy for the overhead lockers the choice is made for you– it goes into the hold. However, there are some good-quality camera cases out there that will protect your kit well.

Look for one that has been drop tested and has clasps that keep shut and preferably with a lock. Lastly many of these cases have small holes in both the top and bottom lips so that when the case is correctly closed they match up. Use a plastic cable tie through these holes and it will make doubly sure that the case cannot come undone accidentally in any event. Don't forget to pack a pair of small snips so that you can cut the ties open when needed (Figures 14.3 and 14.4).

This brings us neatly to another form of protection – insurance. Check the insurance covering the kit you are taking. If you work for a large company ask for the policy details that are applicable to the cover while in transit, and if the camera is going in the hold see if it's covered specifically for this. Ask the airline what insurance cover they give to your kit. It's also worth checking the small print to see if the kit is covered in hotel rooms and in taxis and hire cars. Most insurance companies will have some clauses covering these two situations. They won't pay out if the camera has been stolen after being left on its own in a vehicle, and if it's stolen from a hotel room

FIGURE 14.3
"Pelican cases make tough durable cases suitable for carrying video kit. But it's always good to have a choice and two other makers provide heavy duty boxes Hardigg and Storm case."

FIGURE 14.4
"Cold or what…Who carried that Peli case up there then?…."

they will not cover it if it's in an unlocked room and probably will have more exemption clauses even if the room was locked: They'll certainly want to know who had the room key and where that person was.

Lastly make sure you have personal and third party liability insurance. It needs to be enough to cover legal costs in the country you are going to, and check to see how wide ranging the cover is. Passersby who might trip over your camera box while you concentrate on that lovely sunset could be coerced into making a big deal out of the situation if they could see a pot of money at the end. In the U.K. our filming union, BECTU, offers liability insurance to members at a reduced rate so I'm assuming this is the case with other countries as well.

If you are hiring a kit through a camera facility company they can advise you on many of these points, although they used to provide insurance cover with their kit. Nowadays it's normally the responsibility of the hirer to find insurance cover, and the facility company will want to see the insurance cover note before it let you take the kit abroad.

TIP

If you are doing a lot of flying with the kit you'll already know that some airports expect passengers to walk huge distances from check-in to the plane boarding lounge. We now use a small, lightweight trolley that can fold down to carry the camera and another one for the sound mixer and microphones. This is great for saving your back on these hikes.

Entering some countries with a filming kit requires either a Carnet or item list. The

Carnet system is simply an official transit form that has a sheet for every time you exit customs and enter the next country's customs. On it the name of each item of the filming kit along with its value and individual serial numbers and where the item was bought from are written. It has to be stamped on every exit and entry so that when you return to your home country, the customs people can see that all the items that were taken out of the country at the start of the trip have been brought back in at the end of the trip. They are looking to see if any items have been sold while you were away and if any new items are brought in that were not on the list when you left, then tax will be due on them. At the end of your trip the completed and stamped Carnet needs to be sent back to a designated tax office in your home country.

There is a cost payable for using a Carnet so it's best to check whether the country you intend traveling to really does require the use of one; if it doesn't then it's cheaper to use a simple kit list.

Like the Carnet, it has the name of each item of filming gear along with the value and serial number. You will need to print multiple copies so you can leave one with individual customs officers if required.

If you know in advance that you'll be traveling abroad to film on many occasions throughout a year, the Carnet can be configured to cover multiple trips instead of the one-offs. If you don't feel confident to handle a Carnet there are various agencies and companies that will handle it for you and take care of the details. You then simply provide them with the information about the kit you are taking. Some facilities houses will handle all this for you but again there will be charges. You'll find contact details for these through facility companies, in trade magazines, or on the web.

Carnets are OK but you do have to make sure that each entry and exit post stamps the correct copy so that all the information tallies up when you get back to your home country on the final trip. The only real problem I've encountered is when flying home from Austria half of the equipment did not get put on the plane. The airline apologized and said it would arrive 1 day later, which it did. However, the first half of the kit had gone through customs. So we had to take all the items on the second flight into a customs office miles away from the airport and have it all checked, which costs another day's hire and more admin fees. Luckily all the kit was accounted for and the customs did not fine us.

So you've planned your shoot, you've traveled over to the country, booked into your hotel ready to start shooting after a good night's solid sleep. What on earth could possibly go wrong?… On a trip to Canada to film catfish angling, we decided it would be great to do an aerial shot of the river to set up the program and hired a small plane to do an hour of shooting. We booked it from the U.K. and as we had no contacts we just took the first recommendation we found, which was pleasantly cheaper than we had expected. On arriving at the airfield with the camera I was told to wait in the plane as the pilot would be along shortly and I was shown where to go. The airfield was very, very small, and deserted other than the one guy we had spoken to. I found myself staring at possibly the oldest little Cessna I'd ever seen and started to climb into the passenger seat. The door handle came off in my hand and the door looked like it was going to follow. At this point I realized that we didn't need an aerial shot quite as much as I thought we did and climbed out of the plane's cockpit, being careful not to remove any more parts of the aircraft that might be needed on future flights….

The "What on Earth Can Go Wrong Checklist"

- Confirm that any taxis booked will arrive and know where to go.
- Double-check the time you should allow for journeys to locations.
- Double-check that guests appearing in the shoot know where to go and what time to arrive.
- Make sure the camera kit is working and batteries are charged.
- Put one person in charge of all camera stock.
- Leave extra time to get to locations as planes and taxis can be late and there's nothing you can do but wait.
- Have you bought correct wall sockets/adapters so the battery charger, mains unit, and monitors can all work in the country you are working in?
- Check that all medical matters such as malaria tablets and inoculations have all been completed by the crew before traveling.
- Allow for different time zones.
- Arrange a local guide and fixer when needed.
- Double-check that all permissions and licenses to film have been agreed.

CHAPTER 15

Health and Safety for Location Shooting

PERSONAL CREW SAFETY ON LOCATION...

Some of the points affecting personal safety and the section below on location lighting safety are the same, so please check both categories.

I've no doubt that some readers will have attended safety courses for location camera work and so will be aware of the main issues. In these courses a lot of time is taken up by making people aware of the risks that might affect them before they start filming and making an effort to minimize any risks that are found while shooting. In a way this is the key to location safety, being aware of risks and then doing something positive to reduce them. It's impossible to take all the risks away from shooting or everyday life; even walking down a sidewalk on a sunny day with no one else present is not risk free. You could trip up over a loose paving stone or twist an ankle walking down a curb.

It would be easy to compile a whole book based on today's attitude to health and safety (H&S) and the regulations that cover it, and that book would probably be a lot longer than this one. However, the aim of my book is to help give practical tips and techniques to do with location shooting, so this chapter will continue this and just highlight the main safety issues that filming on location brings. It's down to every crew member to get clued up on H&S and this chapter is not a substitute for researching your local regulations, which can be found on the web.

It's easier to break down the topic into three groups:

1. Planning
2. Risk assessment
3. Controlling the risk while shooting

Planning a safe shoot will make everyone aware of what they will be facing on the filming days and they can then make their own decisions about how to handle it. Correct clothing will be a factor, if the location is outdoors. In the cold or in the rain adequate clothing will be needed. High-visibility jackets will be needed on certain sites as well as hard hats on construction sites. So although this sounds common sense, the fact is that if the crew members aren't told about the need for such clothing then they probably won't bring it along. This should be identified in the risk assessment form and communicated to all crew. Night shoots should always have adequate reflective clothing supplied and extra people to look after the crew's safety as needed. A "back minder" for cameramen filming with a handheld camera and walking backward should also be provided.

If the crew is filming interviews by roads all day someone should order reflective rests for people to wear. Noisy environments need to be flagged up before the day and people should be given ear-defenders or earplugs, if needed, and breaks away from the loud sound on a regular basis.

Anyone who has ridden a motorcycle over long distances without wearing earplugs will tell you about the threat of tinnitus, a permanent buzzing that happens when you are exposed to certain types of loud noise over a prolonged period. If you ever get tinnitus there is nothing you can do about it, it just stays with you. Shooting in cold countries obviously needs correct warm clothing but working in hot climates also brings its challenges. Sunscreens will be needed and it's a good idea to have a remedy for dehydration, which can affect crews working long hours outside in hot countries. You can purchase powders such as dioralyte, which is mixed with water and provides a rehydration system for people suffering

TIP

We found out when shooting our fishing shows around the world that a good source of energy was a normal Coca-Cola that had gone slightly flat after being opened and left for a while. It gives a good boost of sugar and caffeine, which again helps anyone feeling the affect of the sun or after sickness and diarrhea or for when you start flagging during a long day's shooting.

the symptoms. It also helps after sickness and allows fluid to build up again in the body.

FILMING FROM HEIGHT IS ANOTHER RISK

Many accidents occur from falling, so safe access equipment with guard rails erected by professional people is a must, not just for the camera but also the crew. All reasonable personal needs should be catered to, such as an adequate drinking water supply, toilets, heating, etc., and the fact that we work on location should not be used as an excuse not to provide or know where to find these basic amenities.

FILMING IN CARS CAN BE A BIT TRICKY AS WELL

You shouldn't lean out of sunroofs or out of tailgates, and in some countries the police will fine you if they see a camera poking out of a car in what they deem to be a unsafe fashion on a public road. If you film on private land and the production wants you to shoot from these two positions get safety strapping so both you and the camera are secured to the vehicle. If there is a risk employ a competent camera grip with special equipment. Also be aware that shooting from the front passenger seat, let's say your subject is in the rear seat, can be a good way to twist your neck and back, so the use of cameras lighter than a full-blown ENG kit would be useful here. And never film if you feel there is a risk to your safety, just be firm and politely say no. This especially applies if you are asked to go into dangerous situations, and only you know what you can cope with and your limitations. Perhaps you've attended a specialist training course and you are prepared but are the others working with you? I've done a "filming in riots" course and part of the 2 days' training was spent having gas bombs thrown at us while walking toward the throwers…and how to douse the flames when your clothing caught alight. Very scary indeed!

CARRYING A KIT CORRECTLY

A bit less exotic than being gas bombed but no less important for crews is how to lift a kit properly and how to carry the kit it so that it doesn't harm your back. The old adage of bend your knees not your back still holds true here. You can now attend a "manual handling" course that will help identify the risks from picking up and carrying kits. Strangely enough, more sound recordists suffer from bad backs than cameramen. My theory is that it comes from having the sound mixer on a strap around their necks. They operate the mixer standing up but look down at the meters; their neck is bent over, and the weight of the mixer is taken in this position when the back is curved. Some of my friends who complained that this hurt their backs and necks changed to a waist holder, which takes the mixer and accessories on it, and the weight of the kit is carried just above the hips. They use this for walking to and from the location and they then sit down as much as possible when using it and operate the mixer while resting on their knees. You can also get chest harnesses that spread the weight of the mixer across your chest, and strap around the back.

Don't be cajoled into carrying more kit than you find comfortable and therefore more weight than you can happily carry. Everyone is different and has their own limitations in terms of weight carrying, so keep it sensible at all times. If you do expect to carry a kit for long distances get a small fold-up trolley. I use a very lightweight fold-up version that can take all my kit when I'm trudging through large offices or airports from check-in to the boarding gate, as some terminals now have huge walks between these two areas (Figure 15.1).

Cameramen suffer from bad backs because of bad posture brought on by carrying kits and also leaning over the viewfinder for long periods of time. Look at Chapter 16 and the exercises given by physiotherapist Dan Oliver in order to help combat this. Dan has looked at the work location cameramen do and given some stretches and exercises that can be done anywhere: at home, in a hotel room, or while camping by a river bank. If you suffer from a stiff back brought on by filming a deep tissue massage will help relieve the symptoms but if they persist then an osteopath should be consulted to find out where the problem is.

SAFETY WITH LOCATION LIGHTING

There's no escaping H&S issues these days and when you think about it, a video crew entering into other people's offices, houses, and other public locations and plugging in temporary units such as lights, monitors, mains units, and chargers does present a risk for the owners of the property and crew alike. As long as you and your crew have a good idea of how to avoid hazards and incidents while filming, the chances are that you'll all work safely together. It's crews who don't take it seriously or have very little regards for their own and others' safety that present the worst-case scenario. So it's in everyone's benefit to get clued up about procedures that help prevent accidents.

In Chapter 11 we mentioned general location lighting safety using RCD (residual current devices) units between your lamps and the wall sockets

FIG 15.1
Paul's trolley with a kit on it.
"A small lightweight trolley can help crew members on long walks."

FIG 15.2
Paul's RCD unit. "Small compact residual current device that can be used for location filming."

(Figures 15.2 and 15.3) and also running cables under rubber matting or cable ducts when they go across walkways or busy areas (Figure 15.4). Another tip mentioned in the book is to secure lighting stands by hanging a kit bag or sandbag over the bottom legs, which helps stabilize the light in winds or against knocking over.

It also makes sense to have all your lights, cables, and other electrical units tested and checked every year by a competent electrician. If you did have any severe problems with this kit on location the fact you have had a PAT test (portable appliance test) done would definitely help you. A check will also flag up any loose wires, damaged plugs, worn-out components, and other areas that could lead to problems with the kit, allowing you to repair it before it actually breaks down.

You cannot take the entire risk away when working with live electrics but you can minimize it, and one way to avoid injury while using electricity would be by lowering the voltage. But for many video crews, it's difficult to use this strategy on short visits to different locations and while using their standard mains powered lamps.

But one important question that crops up on location and needs an answer is this: *how many mains powered film or video lights can you safely run at one time when you are out shooting?*

FIG 15.3
"This RCD is wired into the cable."

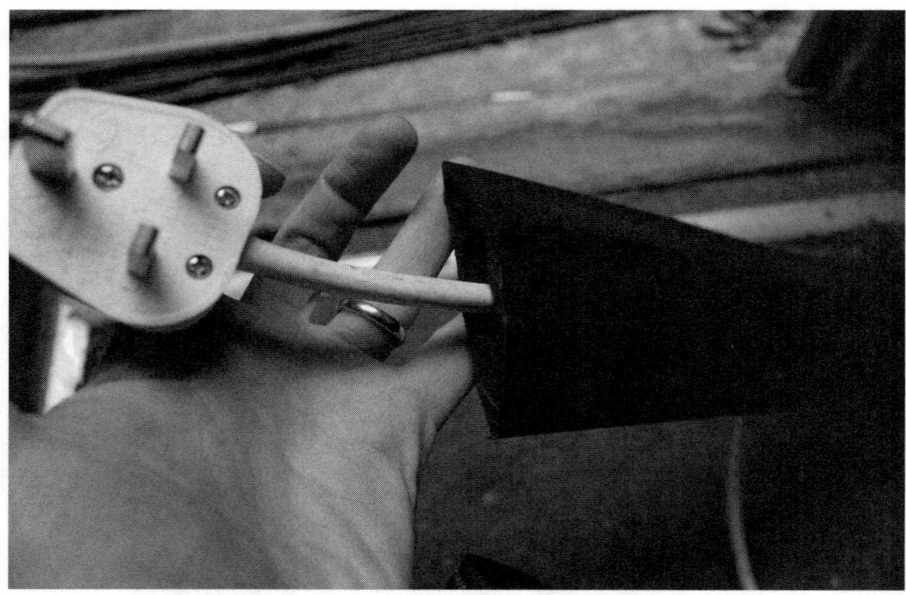

FIG 15.4
Thin rubber ducting for Video crews cables. "This thin rubber ducting holds the cable tight inside it and allows people to tread on it or walk over it without danger of tripping over the open cable."

In the U.K. the domestic circuits are normally 30 amps and this supply is available on a ring main that provides power to individual 13 amp electric sockets. If we take the voltage to be 240 V, running a 1 kW lamp will take 4.2 amps. At 230 V this 1 kW light will take 4.3 amps. So if you are using multiple lamps in a single setup, it's good practice to spread the load between different 13 amp sockets so you do not overload them.

Using the 1 kW light as a reference point of 4.2 amps, you can easily work out the amps taken by your other lamps that are with smaller wattage and come up with a total load amount before plugging everything in. Always check to see what the fuse in each light's plug socket is rated at.

The other point to note with mains powered lights is that they take a higher load when being switched on. This surge dies down when they are on and steady, but if you were to switch all the video lights on at the same time this could prove a problem by overloading the circuit. Extension cables can overheat if they are left coiled up or looped onto their drums and are best used uncoiled. Never run them across doorways or other areas that could trip up people. If you find that you are going to use higher-powered lights that will require more amps on your location shoot, it's advisable to hire an electrician as well. If you do need more power the electrician will advise you on the best way to distribute power for the lighting and handle the day's work. The other factor is that when you end up using larger lights, and more of them, it will slow the actual rate of filming down if the camera operator is doing lights, cables, finding power, etc. as well as filming. Then, again, this could become a safety issue.

Regulations covering the use of the type of equipment we use on location are: Electricity at Work Regulation 1989; which came in force on 1990; the Management of Health and Safety at Work Regulations 1999; and Provision and Use of Work Equipment Regulations 1998.

As many companies, large or small, will not allow lighting equipment to be used on their premises without certificates, it makes sense to have your kit PAT tested and keep up a regular schedule of retests as needed.

Other factors that need to taken into account for location filming safety are:

- How safe the equipment being used is.
- How many other people will be in the area, including the crew, when shooting happens, and will they be near lamps?
- Check all sockets for damage before plugging the video kit in and do not use any that look badly worn, blackened, or cracked.
- Has a risk assessment been done by the production company before the crew arrives and does the crew know about this assessment?
- Always switch off lamps before moving them, and let them cool before handling or packing away.
- Never place lamps directly underneath heat, sprinkler, or smoke sensors.
- If time is tight and the sequence has to be shot quickly in any one location, it can compromise people's safety. Rushing while shooting will always increase the risk of accidents; therefore, always try and avoid situations where stress impacts on safety.
- How much electrical knowledge, or lack of it, does the crew setting up lights have?
- Are any locations using mains powered lights near water, and are the lights going to be positioned by water?
- Does the location have any hazards that might affect lighting or filming equipment or crew? If it does, can another location be found?
- Always ask if the electric sockets are suitable for use before plugging in. Sometimes they are kept separate for other purposes such as computers or other IT equipment.

Some locations will need to have special requirements for lights and other electrical kits. Hospitals will undoubtedly have a set of rules or codes of conduct for anyone bringing in temporary electrical kits. Public venues and other meeting places will also have specific regulations, so it's best to check with the house electricians in any venues like these and get their advice before the filming starts. Some venues will assign an in-house electrician to the crew for the period of filming and they will give you firsthand guidance as to what you can or cannot do. Finally, in the U.K. any users of lights have to comply with the Electricity at Work Act of 1974 because many (mainly large) companies will not allow people without suitable qualifications and training to work with lighting. Even with basic training they will limit users to three lights or 2000 W for indoor use only.

Everyone involved with the shoot has a responsibility for safety and has to be aware of their and their colleagues' safety. Producers and those in similar positions also have a responsibility for safety and they should hire crew members who are competent on location, and the kit hired for the job should also be adequate and safe.

The above information has been taken from U.K. regulations and directives, but every country will have its own set of rules covering this. At the end of the day, no matter what country you are based in, it all comes down to common sense and taking precautions to minimize any risks.

CHAPTER 16

Staying Fit and Well on Location

Shooting as an occupation is physically arduous. Location shooting is even more so as the working days tend to be longer so that producers can get the best out of being in a different setting or country. Add to this the fact that you'll be traveling more, which means hand carrying the kit and coping with more filming problems than normal, and the stress can mount up.

Location shooting has always been physical as we have to carry the kit from place to place: out from the car, into the airports, plus the rigging and de-rigging at each new location. And most cameramen find that this can put a strain on your body that builds up over time. Handheld filming, for instance, can be bad for your back, hips, and spine. A SONY DigiBetacam with large PAG batteries or Anton Bauer batteries will weigh approximately 10–12 kg. Now this unit will balance nicely on your shoulder but it's still heavy, and if you film constantly like this your body will most likely let you know what it thinks and it won't be pleasant…

When you place this much weight on the right-hand side of your body your spine and back compensate by allowing the left side of your back to push up and meet this new mass that's sitting on your shoulder. This compensation also travels down to the hips and legs. Even working with a smaller type of camera like SONY's HVR-Z1e or Canon's XL-1 can put strains on your body, hips, and legs. These cameras don't sit well on your shoulder, so when handholding them you take the weight on your forearms and this pulls your back forward as well, which affects your posture.

Picking up a kit can also be a danger area, especially in the cold, as your body will be less flexible, and this is the time you are likely to pull muscles; in fact, twisting and lifting are the best ways to hurt yourself, so try not to do it.

After many years of physically tiring location shoots abroad and at home I asked physiotherapist Dan Oliver to develop a simple exercise routine that could be easily followed while living in hotels and filming on the road. The idea was to try and work out a short schedule that would keep me fit while working on the road, and when I was back at home, I could add other exercises that would increase my stamina, strength, and flexibility and help protect my back from stiffness and long-term problems. As you look through them you can choose the ones that will help you most; they are all designed to help camerapeople protect themselves against injury and make working life just a bit more pleasant...

EXERCISES

- Split into three areas: stamina, flexibility, and strength.
  You can do simple workouts for your flexibility and strength, even in the smallest of hotel rooms. I do these every morning and do every exercise for thirty seconds, as I don't have the patience to do them for longer. If you find that you are getting frequent stiffness, aches, and general discomfort in your back, shoulders, hips, or legs, try a series of deep tissue massages with a good physiotherapist who should be able to pinpoint the areas that need work. He will also correct any bad posture problems that you are developing from shooting. Tell him what you do and how you stand and work throughout the day. He will pinpoint the areas of your body that need work done to them. A key problem for cameramen is that they lean over the camera all day as well as supporting the camera on their shoulder for hand held work. It's this combination that can affect your posture and lead to back problems.

  All these exercises are recommended by physiotherapist Dan Oliver, who has worked miracles on my back and has recommended them specifically for cameramen (Figure 16.1). Dan demonstrates these below.

Flexibility

- *Cat stretches*:
  Looks after the back muscles. Kneel on the floor with your arms supporting you and your back flat. Then simply push your back upward so there is an arch in your spine. Hold for 30 seconds (Figure 16.2).

FIG 16.1
"Physiotherapist Dan Oliver, who has worked out a simple set of exercises for location crews."

FIG 16.2
Cat stretches.

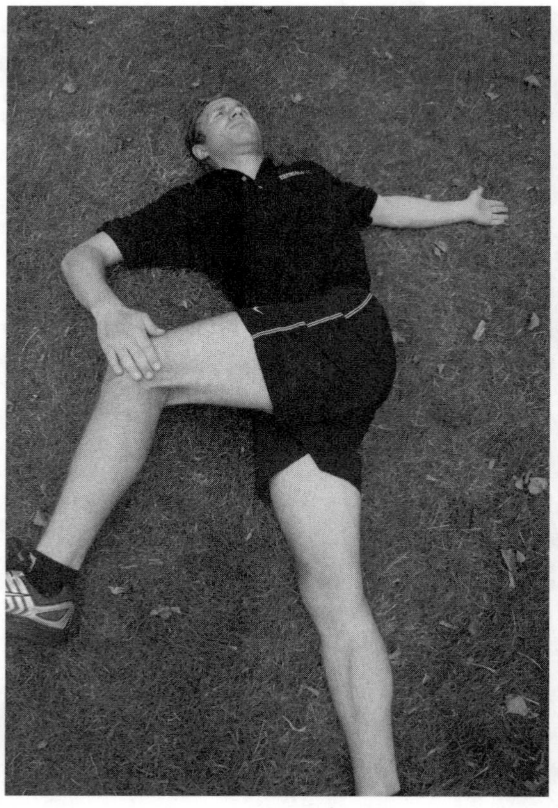

(a)

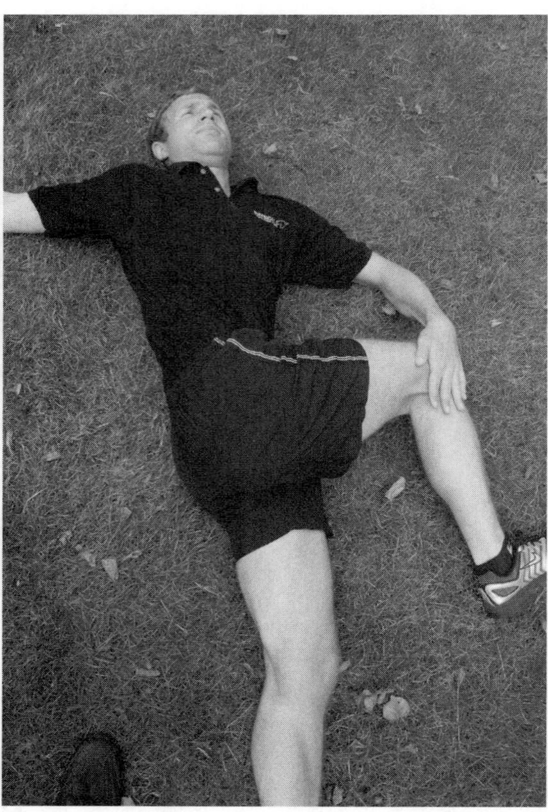

(b)

FIG 16.3
Lower back exercises.

- *Lower back*:
  A good one to help relieve a day of filming and any stiffness in your lower back. As per Figure 16.3a and b, lie on the floor and twist your left leg over to the right-hand side of your body while your left arm remains pointed out to the left side. Do the same for your other side; 30 seconds on each side should do it.
- *Lower back and hips*:
  Stand upright with your legs slightly apart. Slide your left hand and arm down your left side to around the knee area, lifting your right arm up as you go. Hold for 20 seconds, then breathe out and push down a bit further for the next 10 seconds. Repeat for the other side. This is very good to increase your flexibility (Figure 16.4a and b).

(a)

(b)

FIG 16.4
Lower back and hip exercises.

- *Chest and posture*:
  Leaning over cameras all day combined with handheld shooting will do nothing for your posture. And bad posture can lead to back problems. This exercise helps correct round shoulders and pulls them back into line. Stand upright, place your hands on the back of your hips, and push your shoulder blades backward. Hold for 30 seconds (Figure 16.5).
- *Neck stretches*:
  This will help the neck muscles after peering into a viewfinder all day. Stand up straight, hand on right hip, and lean your neck across to the right. Hold for 30 seconds, come back to the upright position, and do the same for the other side (Figure 16.6a and b).

FIG 16.5
Looking after your posture will help protect from back problems.

Strength

My camera kit weighs about 18 kg and I hand carry it to most jobs for 4 days a week. I can cover quite a few miles getting to and from new locations each day if it's busy, so I asked Dan to recommend some exercises that could be done at home and in hotels.

- *Squats*:
  This will help strengthen your legs and make carrying a kit seem easier. As per Figure 16.7a and b, stand straight, arms out, and dip down keeping your spine straight. Don't let your legs splay out as you drop down and keep your ankles in line with your knees.

(a)

(b)

FIG 16.6
Neck stretches.

- *Lunges*:
  Again this will help strengthen the legs. Stand up, hands on hips, put the right leg slightly in front with the left leg pushed out backward, drop the left knee so it's nearly to the ground, and bend the right knee as you go. Hold for a short while, then repeat with the other leg (Figure 16.8a and b).
- *Push-ups*:
  Good old push-ups, you can either do them or not, so they are a good indicator of your upper body strength. If you can do up to 30 in one session, you've got very good upper body strength. When I started doing these a few years ago I found them very hard indeed, so instead of stretching

(a)

(b)

FIG 16.7
Squats for the quadriceps and will help you if you enjoy running as well.

out my legs and resting on my toes (as Dan shows in Figure 16.9a and b) I simply did them on my knees. After a while I had the strength to use the toes method. As Dan shows, keep your back straight and don't flex it too much when coming up.

- *Arm curls*:

  If you have no access to a hotel gym but want to keep your arms in tone for the shoot try this. Get hold of a large PAG battery or a 1 l bottle of water in each hand.

You can also use bags of sugar. Now use these as homemade weights and do simple arm curls. Keep your elbows still and generate the movement from the muscle in your top arm. A 1 l bottle of water weighs 1 kg so you can work out how many repetitions are good for you from this. It doesn't

(a)

(b)

FIG 16.8
As will Lunges.

work if you use cold bottles of beer in each hand because you'll never get to the end of a workout without wanting to drink them…

- *Dips*:
  Good to build up strength in the tops of your arms at the back. Dan uses a Swiss ball to demonstrate but you can also use a chair, bed, or coffee table. Start by leaning your arms back onto the ball/chair and take the weight of your body by bending your knees slightly, then dip down so your arms take more pressure, and push up using your arms (Figure 16.10a and b).

General toning will mean using lighter weights for 12 to 15 repetitions of two to threes sets in each one. To increase strength and muscle size, use heavier

(a)

(b)

FIG 16.9
Push ups for upper body strength.

(a)

(b)

FIG 16.10

weights and try 8 to 10 repetitions with three or four sets. And for pure strength try 1 to 6 repetitions of four to five sets with heavier weights.

Your body's flexibility decreases over time as you get older and also as you get tired. As I said before, if you try and pick up a heavy and cumbersome filming kit when you are cold or tired, you can easily pull muscles. As most location work has a big element of carrying and lifting plus standing around on your feet for most of the day, you need to work on this.

Index